Migration in Britain

Migration in Britain

Paradoxes of the Present, Prospects for the Future

Tony Fielding

University of Sussex, UK

Edward Elgar

Cheltenham, UK • Northampton, MA, USA

Published by
Edward Elgar Publishing Limited
The Lypiatts
15 Lansdown Road
Cheltenham
Glos GL50 2JA
UK

Edward Elgar Publishing, Inc.
William Pratt House
9 Dewey Court
Northampton
Massachusetts 01060
USA

A catalogue record for this book
is available from the British Library

Library of Congress Control Number: 2012930621

ISBN 978 1 78100 419 7

Typeset by Servis Filmsetting Ltd, Stockport, Cheshire
Printed and bound by MPG Books Group, UK

Contents

Acknowledgements

I wish to gratefully acknowledge the financial and practical support of the Government Office for Science Foresight Programme's project on environmental migration for the preparation of the 'drivers of migration' (DR12) report on which Parts II and III of this book are based. I would also like to thank (1) the Foresight team for permission to publish sections of this report; and (2) Elsevier and the editors of *Global Environmental Change*, for permission to publish my 2011 paper entitled 'The impacts of environmental change on UK internal migration', which, in modified versions, form chapters of this book. Finally, I want to thank John Stillwell and his team for helping me with the data used in the opening section of the book, and also anonymous reviewers plus Tony Champion and Russell King for helpful comments on the text.

Introduction

This book is divided into three parts. The first is highly empirical and describes what we know about contemporary internal migration flows in the UK. The second is analytical and largely focuses on the forces shaping internal migration flows in the UK at present and in the recent past; it includes, however, a final chapter that is theoretical and highly speculative and imagines the future trends in internal migration flows in the absence of environmental change. The third, also highly speculative, considers the impact that environmental change might have on these flows.

PART I

UK internal migration patterns

England and Wales: base map of Government Official Regions and of counties selected for special study in Part I of the book

1. Migration: concepts, methods and values

A rich analytical and theoretical literature on internal migration patterns, processes and trends in the UK already exists. This literature will be reviewed, and hopefully extended, in the sections and chapters that follow. The main emphasis of this first part of the book, however, will be on *describing* these patterns and trends, not on identifying their underlying processes or 'drivers'. Therefore, if the reader is not interested in statistical descriptions and does not share this author's enthusiasm for maps and graphs, or alternatively thinks that they know most of the relevant facts already, then they should skip Part I and move directly to Part II.

We know from the Office for National Statistics that about 6 million people in the UK change their place of residence every year. Most of these migrants move only over a very short distance. About 2 million move far enough to cross the borders of the health district (typically counties) in which they live. And about 1 million migrants migrate far enough to cross the borders of the Government's Official Regions (GORs). Three considerations, however, need to be kept in mind: (1) that these figures vary across the business cycle, with higher figures during boom years than in recessions; (2) that the rates of migration per 1000 population have tended to fall or remain roughly steady since the early post-World War II days (despite the class structure shift towards the mobile middle classes and away from the less mobile working classes); and (3) that UK residents are far less migratory than those in some other countries, notably the United States (but see Cooke, 2011).

So what about the origins and destinations of these migrations? It would be reasonable to expect that the dominant flows would be from poor areas to rich ones: specifically, that the highest rates of out-migration would be from the areas with the lowest wages and highest unemployment rates; and that London, in particular, would be a magnet for migrants because that is where wealth and power are concentrated, and where luxury consumption is at its height. But internal migration in the UK is interestingly odd. London loses population through internal migration; especially (can this really be true?) during boom times. And the areas that are poorest and where people face the bleakest of economic futures are also those where out-migration rates are at their lowest. How strange! How intriguing!

But I am running ahead of myself. Some tasks can be rather tedious, but they still have to be done. A discussion of definitions is a case in point. When using the term 'migration' I refer to a change of residence that is at least fairly permanent, and one that implies a move over a significant distance – one that is likely to involve a change of residential environment (such as a move to another town) and might also involve a change of employment (such as a job promotion). It is obvious from this that the boundaries to the concept of 'migration' are not nice and sharp but instead are rather 'fuzzy' – fuzzy in the sense that a temporary migration (such as a working holiday) is often difficult to differentiate from a permanent migration; indeed, temporary migrations quite often 'morph' into permanent ones, in the same way that local suburban or peri-urban residential relocations sometimes morph into 'full' work or lifestyle migrations when, for example, commuting to the city centre ceases on retirement or local employment replaces city centre employment.

Figure 1.1 sets out the broad dimensions of the boundary problems of the concept 'internal migration'. On the left side of the shaded area lie short-distance intra-urban migrations. These are discussed in this book, but do not represent its core focus, despite the fact that several very important and interesting issues arise – notably whether or not there are trends towards greater ethnic segregation in UK city-regions, and if so, what this might mean for the future peace and prosperity of the country. At the lower limit of the shaded area is the boundary between what constitutes a long visit and what constitutes a migration. This boundary has become more significant than previously for two main reasons: the first is the greater proportion of young people who are leaving their home regions for periods of study and training; the second is the growing tendency for young people to engage in temporary out-migration/emigration for work purposes, sometimes captured by the term 'working holiday', and often seen as a vital 'rite of passage' to adulthood – it is an experience that can, for certain individuals and in certain circles, be seen as enhancing their worth (social capital) and social status.

This temporary migration is very typical of much intra-European Union migration, notably of the many migrants from Central and Eastern Europe who came to the UK from eight of the ten countries that joined/accessed the EU in 2004 (the A8 countries). This marks the final fuzzy right-side boundary of internal migration in Figure 1.1. Intra-EU migrations are, in many respects, 'internal migrations' since the crossing of the borders of the member states of the European Union is, to a large extent, legally and practically unencumbered. Europe has (at the time of writing

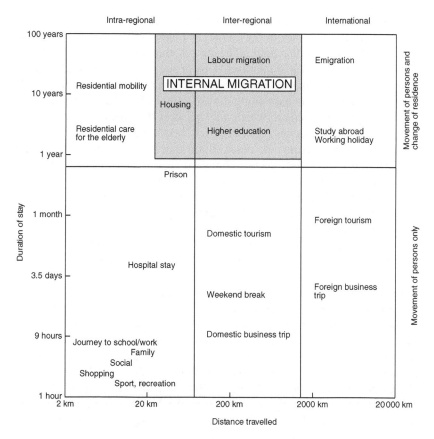

Figure 1.1   Population movements by distance travelled and duration of stay

and to a degree that amazes many people from other parts of the world) a single social and economic space when it comes to the mobility of persons, even for the purposes of work and settlement. But, in this study, the crossing of the UK's international borders will remain defined as an international migration, and only flows within the UK will be defined as internal migration.

Finally, it needs to be said that this book does not concern itself with migrations through the long course of UK history; it confines itself to only those past migrations and their related processes that strongly affect the situation today. So the text will only look back about 50 to 60 years, and will look forward the same length of time towards the second half of the twenty-first century.

So much for operational decisions about 'internal migration' as an object of study. What about the factual evidence? Two datasets are drawn upon in this part of the book. The first is the National Health Service Central Register (NHSCR) dataset. This provides us with annual data, of somewhat dubious quality, but with the advantage that we can see trends over time and what is happening almost now rather than at the time of the last population Census (which may be, as at the time that I am writing this, almost ten years away). The NHSCR data are built upon the fact that when people move from one place to another they tend to change their doctors (but even if they do not change their doctors they are supposed to inform the NHS that they have changed their place of residence). The place of former residence and the place of current residence are recorded as they register with their new GP (general practitioner), and this information is centralized in the NHSCR. A couple of problems are immediately apparent: first, sick people are more dependent upon medical help than healthy ones, and so certain groups of people, notably young adult males who have, or think they have, less need for medical help, tend not to register with a new GP when they migrate from one place to another; second, and clearly related to this, there is, more generally, a time lag between migrating and registering. Nevertheless, where we can compare the NHSCR data with Census data (for example, for migration during the year prior to the Census) it turns out that the two datasets tell very much the same story (Boden, 1989; Smallwood and Lynch, 2010; Stillwell et al., 2010, but see also Jivraj and Marquis, 2009 and Raymer et al., 2011). This encourages us to be fairly confident that the NHSCR data are, broadly speaking, telling us the truth about internal migration flows in the UK (at least at spatial scales above that of the very local).

In the pages that follow I use the NHSCR dataset for the year up to 31 March 2010 (June 2009 in Scotland). This has the big advantage that it is, at the time of writing, pretty up-to-date. It has the big disadvantage, however, that it covers a year that was quite extraordinary in comparison with the 12 years that preceded it (but may not turn out to be so extraordinary in comparison with the years to come). It was a year of severe recession and partial bounce-back following the near collapse of the Western financial system in September 2008. As we shall discover, the recession left many migration processes remarkably untouched, but, due to the special circumstances of the housing and labour markets in that year, it would be foolish to generalize about internal migration patterns in the UK on the basis of this one source of information alone.

For this reason, not only do I use NHSCR data for other years as well, but more significantly, I draw upon the Special Migration Statistics dataset from the 2001 Census. This provides both a broad back-up picture of contemporary internal migration in the UK from a completely different source, and also a snapshot of migration flows during a period of relative economic stability, when both housing and labour markets were buoyant, and confidence in the economy was high. The Census data are produced by a question that asks each person in the household where they lived one year prior to the Census date. The flow data that result can be mapped and analysed at both the level of the Government's Official Regions and at the county level. Since the NHSCR data are also available at these levels, a close, although not exact, comparison can be made between the patterns for 2000–01 and those for 2009–10.

How is all this data analysed? Economists (and some economic geographers) would be inclined to put the migration flow data into a linear regression equation with migration from origin i to destination j ($Mi - j$), as the dependent (y) variable (that is, the variable to be explained), and with 'gravity model' variables (Pi = population at origin, Pj = population at destination, $Di - j$ = distance between origin and destination), plus economic variables (notably income per capita and unemployment differences between i and j) as the independent (x) variables (that is, the things that cause the variations in the y variable – the migration flows). I have, for two main reasons, decided against this approach. The reasons are: (1) I judge it likely, on the basis of previous work, that the social class (e.g., occupational status, educational level) characteristics of both migrants and places will be important in explaining outcomes. This is difficult, if not impossible, to incorporate satisfactorily into a linear model. And (2) what if it turns out that there is not just one system or 'nexus' of migration–society links, but rather several systems that coexist? In a linear model it is usual for everything to be conflated, and for all these crucially important differences to be lost.

My approach, therefore, is to use 'rich description'; that is, to process the data in ways that reveal as much as possible about the people and places involved while 'staying close to the data'. I do this by using 'migration velocities' to measure the size of flows from particular origins to particular destinations, and by using 'location quotients' to highlight the age characteristics of the inter-area in-migrants at particular destinations, and of the out-migrants at particular origins. Migration velocities were first used, to my knowledge, by Kono and Shio in their monograph on inter-prefectural migration flows in Japan (Kono and Shio, 1965). A migration velocity (mv) is calculated by dividing the specific migration flow $Mi - j$ by the product of the populations at i and at j ($Pi * Pj$). It can be best understood, therefore, as a kind of standardized rate – hence 'velocity' – of migration flow; standardized, that is, by the sizes of the populations at both origin and destination. Since one is standardizing for the sizes of the populations at origin and destination, it would not be surprising, perhaps, if the migration velocity values would cluster strongly around a mean value. But this is most certainly not the case. As we shall see, the values of *mv* not only reflect the tendency for people to migrate more over shorter distances than over longer ones, they also reflect the deep-rooted historical, cultural and social characteristics and network connections of places, as well as the locations of income, employment and occupational promotion opportunities in the space economy (the full matrix of inter-county migration velocities for 2009–10 can be obtained from the author). Their particular strength is that they greatly assist comparison, not only across a spatial system at a point in time, but also from one period to another.

Location quotients were first used in studies of the links between interregional migration and regional economic growth at about the same time as migration velocities appeared (Fielding, 1966). A location quotient (lq) measures the ratio of the local or regional percentage value of a variable to the national percentage value for the same variable. In this section, for example, the proportion of migrants to destination j who are aged 15–19 ($Mj15-19 * 100/Mj$), is divided by the proportion of migrants to all destinations who are aged 15–19 ($Msumj15-19 * 100/Msumj$) (the full set of in-migrants' age location quotients for 2009–10 can be obtained from the author). So the location quotient, as used here, highlights the distinctiveness of particular origins and destinations with respect to the age compositions of their out- and in-migration flows.

So much for concepts and methods. What about values? The judgement of the author is that migration really matters. It transforms people's lives, sometimes for the worse (for example, when migration is experienced as being 'crippled inside'), but often for the better (for example, when migration is experienced as a 'stairway to heaven') (Fielding, 1992c); and it transforms the cities and regions from which the migrants leave and those to which the migrants go. How could London, for example, have become the amazingly multi-ethnic, hyper-energetic, ultra socially polarized place that it is, without the large, class-, age- and lifestyle-selective gross in-, out- and net migrations of its UK-born population, and also the massive, diverse gross in-, out- and net migrations of its non-UK-born population? We need, in short, to understand migration in order to be able to understand both contemporary UK/British society as a whole, and its shifting, richly varied internal human geography.

2. Inter-regional migration

Table 2.1 provides us with an overview of the internal migration situation in 2009–10 (please note that the countries of Scotland, Wales and Northern Ireland are treated as 'regions' of the UK; please note also that all these tables are subject to rounding errors).

A number of very important facts can be extracted from this table:

- Just over 1 million people migrated between regions in the year to March 2010, and about 20 per cent of these migrations involved London (which is just 12.5 per cent of the UK population).
- By far and away the largest in- and out-migration rates were found in the southern and eastern regions of the UK, with the regions having the largest in-rates also having the largest out-rates (see below).
- The single largest net flow, both in absolute numbers and in terms of rates, was the out-migration flow from London.
- This loss was not just to the surrounding regions of south-eastern UK (East and South East) – the three regions together also slightly lost population through migration to the rest of the UK.
- However, if one considers the Severn–Wash line as demarcating the North/South divide, there was a small net gain to the 'South' from the 'North'.
- The regions of the industrial Midlands and North (West Midlands, North West, Yorkshire & Humber and North East) lost by internal migration.
- Three of the four peripheral regions of the UK (South West, Wales, Northern Ireland and Scotland) had net gains (the exception being Northern Ireland) with the South West having the largest rate of net gain in the UK (even larger than for the South East and East regions).
- Finally, the gross in- and out-migration rates for Scotland and Northern Ireland were quite remarkably low.

Table 2.1   UK internal migration 2009–10: regional migration rates

	Population in 1000s in 2009	In-migration in 1000s 2009–10	Out-migration in 1000s 2009–10	Net migration in 1000s 2009–10	In-migration Rate per 1000	Out-migration Rate per 1000	Net migration Rate per 1000
Scotland	5194.0	45.7	41.5	4.2	8.8	8.0	0.8
N. Ireland	1788.9	10.6	11.3	-0.7	5.9	6.3	-0.4
Wales	2999.3	49.8	48.3	1.5	16.6	16.1	0.5
North East	2584.3	37.5	39.5	-2.0	14.5	15.3	-0.8
North West	6897.9	95.7	102.8	-7.1	13.9	14.9	-1.0
Yorks & Humber	5258.1	89.5	95.3	-5.8	17.0	18.1	-1.1
E. Midlands	4451.2	101.2	95.0	6.2	22.7	21.3	1.4
W. Midlands	5431.1	88.4	98.0	-9.6	16.3	18.0	-1.8
East	5766.6	132.3	119.2	13.1	22.9	20.7	2.3
London	7753.6	178.2	219.0	-40.8	23.0	28.2	-5.3
South East	8435.7	209.1	187.3	21.8	24.8	22.2	2.6
South West	5231.2	123.7	104.5	19.2	23.6	20.0	3.7
UK	61791.9	1161.7	1161.7	0.0	18.8	18.8	0.0

Sources: National Health Service Central Register (NHSCR) and Office for National Statistics (ONS).

Table 2.2   UK population change 2008–09: regional natural increase and total (i.e., internal plus international) migration rates

	Population in 1000s in 2009	Net Natural Increase 2008–09 1000s	Net Total Migration 2008–09 1000s	Net Population Increase 2008–09 1000s	Natural Increase Rate per 1000	Net Migration Rate per 1000	Population Increase Rate per 1000
Scotland	5 194.0	4.6	20.9	25.5	0.9	4.0	4.9
N. Ireland	1 788.9	10.6	3.3	13.9	5.9	1.8	7.7
Wales	2 999.3	3.3	5.9	9.2	1.1	2.0	3.1
North East	2 584.3	2.9	10.7	13.6	1.1	4.1	5.2
North West	6 897.9	17.8	6.0	23.8	2.6	0.9	3.5
Yorks & Humber	5 258.1	16.1	24.5	40.6	3.1	4.7	7.8
E. Midlands	4 451.2	11.8	10.1	21.8	2.7	2.3	5.0
W. Midlands	5 431.1	19.7	3.0	22.7	3.6	0.6	4.2
East	5 766.6	19.1	30.1	49.3	3.3	5.2	8.5
London	7 753.6	78.5	6.8	85.2	10.1	0.9	11.0
South East	8 435.7	27.2	40.0	67.2	3.2	4.7	7.9
South West	5 231.2	4.9	15.9	20.9	0.9	3.0	3.9
UK	61 791.9	216.5	177.2	393.7	3.5	2.9	6.4

Source: ONS components of population change estimates.

Table 2.2 provides us with an overview of the components of UK population change in 2008–09.

This table shows that:

- Both natural increase (births minus deaths) and net international migration made major contributions to the modest overall growth of the UK population in 2008–09 (0.64 per cent).
- Rates of natural increase were particularly important in London (due largely to the low number of deaths) and in Northern Ireland (due to the high number of births).
- Total migration (internal, international and armed forces) was especially important in the East and South East regions, but also in Yorkshire & Humber, North East and Scotland.
- The net international migration gain to London was so large that it more than compensated for the large net internal migration loss (see below).
- Despite 2008–09 being a recession year, and that the recession had been caused by a financial crisis, the highest rate of population increase (+11.0 per 1000) was in the UK's (and Europe's) financial capital, London.

Unlike the above, Table 2.3 uses Census data to provide an overview of the regional patterns on internal migration in the UK. The data refers to inter-regional migration in the year prior to the 2001 Census.

This table shows that:

- The overall level of mobility and the broad patterns of flows are very conformable with the equivalent data obtained from the NHSCR for 2009–10. The UK gross in- and out-migration rates per 1000 population are 18.8 for the NHSCR data and 18.7 for the Census data, and the correlations between the two sets of data are +0.99, +0.98 and +0.90 for the gross in-, gross out- and net in-migration rates respectively. Clearly, despite the different dates and the very different methods of data collection, we are recording, broadly speaking, a single reality of UK internal migration.
- The differences, although minor, are interesting: first, in line with the fact that 2000–01 was a period of relative buoyancy in the labour and housing markets, the net migration loss to London was higher both in absolute terms (51 100 over 40 800) and in rate per 1000 population (−6.9 over −5.3) that year than in 2009–10; second, that this movement away from London was not confined to the Greater London area – the South East Government Official Region (GOR),

Table 2.3   UK internal migration 2000–01: regional migration rates

	Population in 1000s in 2001	In-migration in 1000s 2000–01	Out-migration in 1000s 2000–01	Net migration in 1000s 2000–01	In-migration Rate per 1000	Out-migration Rate per 1000	Net migration Rate per 1000
Scotland	5115	47.8	46.9	1.0	9.3	9.2	0.2
N. Ireland	1698	10.9	11.8	−0.9	6.4	6.9	−0.5
Wales	2946	50.0	44.5	5.5	17.0	15.1	1.9
North East	2577	35.0	37.2	−2.2	13.6	14.4	−0.9
North West	6894	89.3	96.0	−6.7	12.9	13.9	−1.0
Yorks & Humber	5058	89.8	84.1	5.8	17.8	16.6	1.1
E. Midlands	4208	102.1	86.4	15.6	24.3	20.5	3.7
W. Midlands	5335	83.9	90.6	−6.7	15.7	17.0	−1.3
East	5460	128.8	118.4	10.4	23.6	21.7	1.9
London	7375	154.5	205.5	−51.1	20.9	27.9	−6.9
South East	8115	202.8	196.9	5.9	25.0	24.3	0.7
South West	4975	124.3	100.8	23.5	25.0	20.3	4.7
UK	59756	1119.0	1119.0	0.0	18.7	18.7	0.0

Source: 2001 Census.

which wraps around London on its southern and western sides, was assuredly a major net gainer from London (+27 300), but was also a major net loser to the South West and East Midlands regions (−12 500 and −5600 respectively).

- As sometimes happens in periods of economic growth, the 'drift to the South' was reversed – the net gains of the regions (other than London) located south of the line drawn from the Severn to the Wash (+39 800) were overshadowed by the losses of London itself (−51 100), resulting in a net northward migration of 11 300.

Finally, Table 2.4 sets out the components of population change in 2000–01.
A number of very important facts can be extracted from this table and from the statistics (not shown here) that lie behind the data in the table:

- London was, around the turn of the millennium, experiencing very rapid population growth (at least by UK standards). This was a product of both high net immigration (which, at +132 800, far more than compensated the high net internal migration loss of −68 600) and high natural increase (which resulted, not from high fertility, but from the youthfulness of the adult population, which in turn arose from the age-selective nature of its in- and out-migration flows).
- All but one of the other regions with high population growth rates were located in the south and east of the UK, and that their high rates resulted from high net (mostly internal) migration gain.
- The exception was Northern Ireland where the youthful age structure resulting in high natural increase was a product of high fertility (a total fertility rate of 1.83 compared with a UK figure of 1.63).
- Finally, there was a marked negative correlation between net internal migration rates and net international migration rates (−0.83). This was massively affected by the situation in London where the rate of net internal migration was −9.3 per 1000 population, and the net international migration rate was +18.0 per 1000 (please note that the components of change estimates, which are based on the NHSCR migration data, give slightly different absolute and rate figures from those of the Census).

Finally, the 2000–01 Census data can be used to see if there are any significant differences between males and females in their inter-regional migration rates. Perhaps rather surprisingly, the differences are extremely slight; there is a small bias towards men migrating longer distances and women migrating shorter distances, and London tends to have fairly

Table 2.4 Components of population change 2000–01

	Population in 1000s in 2001	Net Natural Increase 2001 1000s	Net Total Migration 2000–01 1000s	Net Population Increase 2000–01 1000s	Natural Increase Rate per 1000	Net Migration Rate per 1000	Population Increase Rate per 1000
Scotland	5 115	−4.9	0.3	−4.6	−1.0	0.1	−0.9
N. Ireland	1 698	7.5	−0.7	6.8	4.4	−0.4	4.0
Wales	2 946	−2.4	6.9	4.5	−0.8	2.3	1.5
North East	2 577	−2.2	−0.2	−2.4	−0.9	−0.1	−0.9
North West	6 894	0.6	2.1	2.7	0.1	0.3	0.4
Yorks & Humber	5 058	3.8	17.0	20.8	0.8	3.4	4.1
E. Midlands	4 208	2.1	17.3	19.4	0.5	4.1	4.6
W. Midlands	5 335	6.9	4.0	10.9	1.3	0.7	2.0
East	5 460	6.8	27.1	33.9	1.2	5.0	6.2
London	7 375	46.0	64.2	110.2	6.2	8.7	14.9
South East	8 115	9.1	22.2	31.3	1.1	2.7	3.9
South West	4 975	−5.5	29.7	24.2	−1.1	6.0	4.9
UK	59 756	66.8	189.9	256.7	1.1	3.2	4.3

Source: ONS components of change estimates.

balanced in-migration flows, but has out-migration flows that are biased towards women (but see also Dennett and Stillwell, 2010).

To summarize, although position in the business cycle does make a difference, the broad features of UK internal migration at the regional level in the 2000s are as follows:

1. London is in a class of its own as a major net loser by internal migration (but a major net gainer by international migration).
2. The regions of southern and eastern England are both net gainers by internal migration and regions of high population turnover.
3. The regions of northern and western UK are both regions of low gains or losses and regions of low population turnover.
4. Internal migration is the major component in population change in most regions (the exceptions being London and Northern Ireland where natural increase is also very important).

3. A more detailed regional, sub-regional (county-level) and occasionally city-level analysis

3.1 SCOTLAND

Table 3.1 summarizes the migration and components of change data for the broad regions of Scotland in the years 2000–01 and 2008–09.

A couple of very important facts can be extracted from this table. First, that there has been a significant shift in the Scottish demographic situation towards population growth, driven especially by migration. Second, that whereas in 2000–01 the migration gains were mostly in the south of the country with losses in the north, in 2008–09 the gains were everywhere but especially in the east. At the core of the East Central region is the Lothian sub-region (containing Edinburgh), which in 2008–09 had the highest sub-regional rate of natural increase (due largely to its high young adult population) and, along with Grampian, the highest rate of net migration gain. There are signs here that Lothian/Edinburgh is showing, on a much smaller scale, some of the same demographic features that characterize London. The third highest rate of net migration gain is recorded by Tayside sub-region, which is also located in the East Central region.

A more detailed picture of these recent migration patterns can be obtained in Table 3.2. This table provides data at the council administrative level on gross in-, out- and net migration rates for migration within Scotland, net migration rate for migration exchanges with the rest of the UK and net migration rate for exchanges with the rest of the world.

A number of striking conclusions can be drawn from this table:

- As with England and Wales (see below), there is a strong positive correlation between gross in- and gross out-migration rates for internal migrations within Scotland. The areas with unusually low in- and out-rates tend to be in the industrial west of Scotland (notably North Lanarkshire and Inverclyde), but low rates also characterize Dumfries & Galloway in the Borderlands and Fife in the East Central region. The areas with unusually high in- and out-rates

Table 3.1 Scotland: regional migration and population changes 2000–01 and 2008–09

	Population 1000s in 2000	Natural Increase Rate per 1000 2000–01	Net Migration Rate per 1000 2000–01	Population Increase Rate per 1000 2000–01	Population in 1000s in 2008	Natural Increase Rate per 1000 2008–09	Net Rate per 1000 2008–09	Population Increase Rate per 1000 2008–09
Highland & Is	277.1	−1.4	−1.0	−2.4	287.5	0.5	4.8	4.8
Grampian	527.4	0.3	−3.2	−2.9	539.7	2.2	9.1	10.1
East Central	1794.6	−0.4	1.9	1.1	1867.3	1.6	5.9	7.5
West Central	2204.9	−1.0	3.2	2.5	2213.2	0.3	1.8	2.1
Borderlands	254.0	−2.7	5.5	2.8	261.0	−1.5	2.1	0.7
Scotland	5058.2	−0.8	2.0	1.2	5168.7	0.9	4.2	4.9

Note: Please note that the figures in columns 4 and 8 are adjusted for changes in armed forces, and that the totals do not conform exactly to the figures in Tables 2.2 and 2.4 in Chapter 2.

Sources: Office for National Statistics (ONS) components of change estimates and National Health Service Central Register (NHSCR).

tend to be middle-class suburban and peri-urban areas (such as the in-rates for East Lothian and Midlothian near Edinburgh), and the university cities (notably Stirling and Aberdeen, but also Dundee, Edinburgh and Glasgow).

- Net internal migration within Scotland tends to reflect three patterns – first, the migration from major cities towards their suburban and peri-urban districts (for example, Edinburgh City loses, and Midlothian and East Lothian gain; Aberdeen City loses, and Aberdeenshire gains); second, the losses from heavy industry districts (such as Inverclyde); and finally, the losses from peripheral rural and remote districts (such as the Orkney Islands, Western Isles/Eilean Siar and Argyll and Bute).

- In stark contrast, net migration exchanges with the rest of the UK favour two kinds of areas: first, the remote north and west (notice the remarkably high rates of net gain for the Orkney and Shetland Islands, and the high rates for the Western Isles, Highlands, Moray and Argyll and Bute); and second, the areas close to the border with England (gains for both Dumfries & Galloway and the Scottish Borders).

- Exchanges with non-UK origins and destinations are not only significant because they produce a large net migration gain for Scotland as a whole (representing about 12 per cent of the total UK net gain), but because they display an extremely distinctive geography. The net gains for Aberdeen City (+17.0 per 1000) and for the City of Edinburgh (+11.7 per 1000) are truly remarkable, but also impressive are the rates of gain for Perth and Kinross, Glasgow and Dundee cities, and Stirling.

- Finally, these patterns intersect in an interesting and intriguing way. The UK immigrants go to one set of places that the Scots are leaving (the central cities of the main city-regions); the 'rest of UK' migrants go to another (this time to the remote areas of northern and western Scotland). The correlation coefficients for these pairings are negative: that between within Scotland net internal migration rates and those for the rest of UK internal migration is –0.27; that between within Scotland net migration rates and those for UK immigration is –0.32. There is also a small negative relationship (–0.11) between the net migration rates for the rest of UK migrants and UK immigrants. One might perhaps be forgiven for imagining that these three groups of migrants were playing a complex game of mutual avoidance!

The NHSCR data can also help us discover something about the migrants to (and from) Scotland from (and to) the rest of the UK. Figures 3.1a and 3.1b show the age structures of in-migrants to, and out-migrants

Table 3.2   Migration within Scotland, with the rest of the UK, and to/from outside the UK

	Population in 1000s in 2008	Gross In-migration Rate 2008–09 per 1000	Gross Out-migration Rate 2008–09 per 1000	Net Intra-Scotland Rate 2008–09 per 1000	Net Rest of UK Rate 2008–09 per 1000	Net Immigration Rate 2008–09 per 1000
Shetland Islands	22.0	17.4	16.9	0.6	5.3	2.0
Orkney Islands	19.9	17.7	20.8	-3.2	8.4	-1.2
Eilean Siar	26.2	22.8	24.0	-1.2	4.0	-0.7
Highlands	219.4	18.8	18.5	0.4	3.4	1.1
Moray	87.8	19.3	18.5	0.8	4.4	0.2
Aberdeenshire	241.5	23.1	20.2	2.9	1.1	2.0
Aberdeen City	210.4	27.4	32.2	-4.8	1.5	17.0
Angus	110.3	21.1	21.2	-0.2	0.3	0.8
Dundee City	142.5	25.4	26.0	-0.6	-0.2	6.4
Perth and Kinross	144.2	23.9	21.5	2.4	1.8	8.2
Fife	361.9	15.7	15.0	0.7	0.6	1.8
Stirling	88.4	32.0	33.4	-1.4	1.4	3.8
Clackmannan	50.5	23.2	23.2	0.0	0.2	0.1
Falkirk	151.6	17.6	14.8	2.8	0.0	0.6
West Lothian	169.5	19.3	19.4	-0.1	-1.2	2.0
Edinburgh City	471.6	23.0	24.7	-1.8	0.8	11.7
Midlothian	80.6	27.6	21.1	6.5	-0.5	-0.1
East Lothian	96.1	26.6	22.0	4.6	0.9	1.4
Argyll & Bute	90.5	22.8	26.5	-3.7	3.3	-1.2
Inverclyde	80.8	10.6	14.2	-3.5	-0.6	-0.6
Renfrewshire	169.8	19.6	18.7	0.9	-0.4	0.5
W. Dunbarton	90.9	19.2	19.1	0.2	-0.2	0.0

E. Dunbarton	104.7	25.0	25.0	0.0	−0.2	−0.4
E. Renfrewshire	89.2	27.7	26.2	1.4	−0.5	−0.6
Glasgow City	584.2	23.8	26.4	−2.6	0.0	6.5
N. Lanarkshire	325.5	15.2	15.3	0.0	0.1	−0.1
S. Lanarkshire	310.1	19.3	16.8	2.5	−0.2	−0.6
North Ayrshire	135.9	18.4	19.7	−1.2	0.9	−1.3
East Ayrshire	119.9	21.2	17.9	3.3	0.9	−1.5
South Ayrshire	111.7	20.8	19.7	1.1	1.7	−1.4
Scottish Borders	112.4	20.3	18.9	1.4	2.1	−0.3
Dumfries & Galloway	148.6	11.5	12.1	−0.6	3.6	−1.7
Scotland	5168.7	21.0	21.0	0.0	0.8	3.1

Sources: ONS estimates and NHSCR.

from, Scotland in 2009–10. In each case the columns are proportional in area to the absolute number of migrants in each age group (this is achieved by making the width of the column equal to that age group's share of all internal migrants), and the height of the column indicates the situation in Scotland relative to all inter-district internal migrants in the UK (a location quotient of 1.0 represents the national figure).

One can see straight away that the in-migration flow to Scotland is positively biased in two respects: first, there are rather more 15–19-year-old in-migrants than average (very likely English students studying at Scottish universities), and second, there are many more in-migrants aged in their 40s, 50s and 60s. Undoubtedly, some of these are returnees – men and women who have spent part of their lives working and living in the UK outside Scotland who now return to the country of their birth and upbringing later in their working-age lives. But it is also likely that some (though probably only a small proportion) of these people are the English migrants to northern and western Scotland discussed in the section above.

The profile for out-migrants also has two distinctive features: first, there is a marked lack of out-migrants aged 15–19, suggesting that Scottish school leavers tend to study, train and enter employment in Scotland. Second, there tends to be a slight tendency for people to leave Scotland in their 20s. In addition to the returning students, this might reflect the many work opportunities south of the border, and in particular, perhaps, the good promotion prospects in London (see Chapter 4, Section 4.4 on the subject of 'escalator region').

Finally, Figure 3.1c shows the net migration balance for migration flows between Scotland and the rest of the UK in 2009–10. This time, the base line is the age structure of the population of Scotland, and the age-specific rates are per 1000 population in that age group. This means that the areas of the columns once again are proportional to the absolute numbers involved. Figure 3.1c reinforces what was described above. The net gain in the 15–19 age group is now even clearer, but the losses in the 20s and the gains thereafter are also clear. The rates of gain and loss are noticeably modest. This is hardly surprising given the large size of Scotland's population (about 10 per cent of the population of the UK), and the distances that separate Scotland's main centres of population and employment from those of the rest of the UK.

3.2 NORTHERN IRELAND

We can now use similar methods to discover the key characteristics of Northern Ireland's internal migration flows. Figures 3.2a and 3.2b

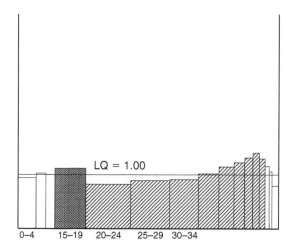

Source: NHSCR.

Location quotients: UK = 1.00

Figure 3.1a *The age structure of internal migration flows to Scotland from the rest of the UK in 2009–10*

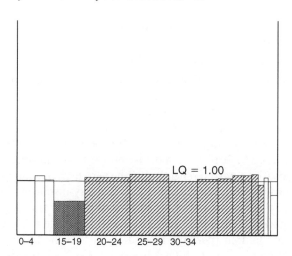

Source: NHSCR.

Location quotients: UK = 1.00

Figure 3.1b *The age structure of internal migration flows from Scotland to the rest of the UK in 2009–10*

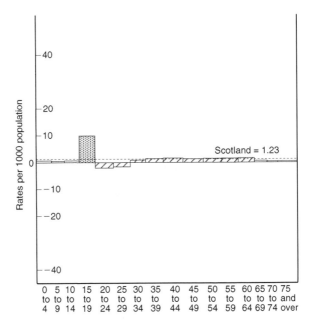

Source: NHSCR.

Figure 3.1c   *Net (UK) internal migration by age group for Scotland in*
             2009–10

likewise have some distinctive features. First, there is a marked lack of
in-migration of the 15–19 age group, which suggests, among other things,
an unattractiveness of Northern Ireland universities to students from
Britain. In fact, there are three times as many students from the Republic
of Ireland (3240) studying in Northern Ireland as there are from Britain
(1025) (UK: HESA, 2010). Second, the bias towards in-migration in the
20–24 age group is a partial reflection of the very high out-migration in the
15–19 age group. These are likely to be, in many instances, the students
returning to Northern Ireland after periods of study or training in Britain.
The other marked features of the out-migration profile are the low levels
of outflow of children (perhaps related in part to the larger families in
Northern Ireland leading to higher housing costs in destination regions),
and the remarkably low levels of outflow of older adults, especially the
retired. This reflects perhaps not only the cultural ties and social class
composition of the middle-aged and older people of Northern Ireland, but
probably also their smaller pensions and less accumulated wealth, both of
which would inhibit pre-retirement and retirement migration.

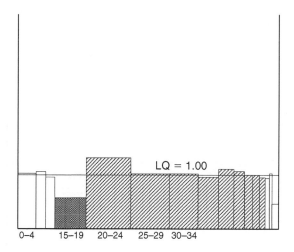

Source: NHSCR.

Location quotients: UK = 1.00

Figure 3.2a   *The age structure of internal migration flows to Northern Ireland from the rest of the UK in 2009–10*

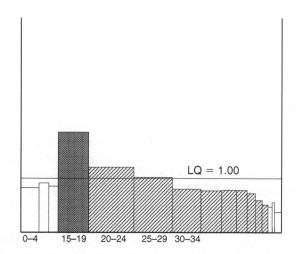

Source: NHSCR.

Location quotients: UK = 1.00

Figure 3.2b   *The age structure of internal migration flows from Northern Ireland to the rest of the UK in 2009–10*

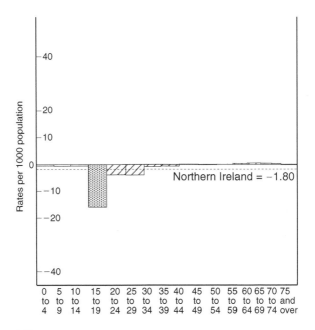

Source: NHSCR.

*Figure 3.2c   Net (UK) internal migration by age group for Northern
Ireland in 2009–10*

Figure 3.2c confirms that, in a context of near equality of inflows and
outflows or of small overall net loss (–1.80 per 1000 population), Northern
Ireland is, above all, losing its young adults, especially those aged 15–19,
but also those in their 20s. This is by no means the whole story, however.
First, as was the case in Scotland, within Northern Ireland there was both
a pattern of migration from city centres to suburban and peri-urban areas,
along with losses from some (mostly western) rural districts. Second, the
major migration event of the 2000s in Northern Ireland was not its within-
province migration, nor its Britain/Northern Ireland exchanges, but the
sizeable net immigration gain from outside the UK. Over the five years
from mid-2004, a net gain of 34 000 persons occurred, mostly young adults
coming from the A8 countries of Central and Eastern Europe. In fact,
37 per cent of Northern Ireland's foreign-born population arrived in the
province in just four years between 2004 and 2007; this is the highest figure
in the UK (Reid and Miller, 2010–11). And data for 2008–09 show that
they did not, for the most part, settle in Belfast, but rather in the small and
medium-sized towns of the central, southern and south-eastern parts of

the province (for example, Dungannon, Craigavon and Newry) (NISRA, 2010). It remains to be seen how much of this migration has become permanent settlement.

3.3 ENGLAND AND WALES

Before examining in more detail the situations in specific regions in England and Wales, this section provides an overview of the main patterns at the county level for the whole country.

Figures 3.3a and 3.3b show the gross in- and out-migration rates for 2009–10. The main features are as follows:

- Quite clearly, the rates of both in- and out-migration are higher in the South and East than they are in the North and West.
- London, despite its location in the high turnover South of England, has relatively low rates in both cases. Large conurbations tend to have lower rates of in- and out-migration than their surrounding areas.
- The exceptions to low rates in the North and West tend to be the more rural, middle-class areas such as North Yorkshire, Lincolnshire, Cheshire, Herefordshire and Mid-Wales. The equivalent maps for 2000–01 (not shown here), although based on the Census and not the NHSCR, are extremely similar.

The striking positive correlation between in- and out-migration rates, flying as it does in the face of standard economic theory (which predicts an inverse relationship such that places that are poor have high out-migration rates and low in-migration rates, and vice versa), is shown in Figure 3.4. Clearly, population size and relative location (Fotheringham, 1991) play a role in producing this result, but the main factors are related to occupational social class, and reflect the social capitals, spatial networks, and triple biographies (work, social/family and place identities) of the inhabitants (see Chapters 5–7).

Figures 3.5a and 3.5b take this analysis one stage further. They show the net migration rates for intra-UK migration by county for 2009–10 (NHSCR data) and 2000–01 (Census). There are many common features to the two maps:

- London is the major loser on both occasions, with the West Midlands a close second in 2009–10.
- Rural areas in southern and eastern England are the major gainers

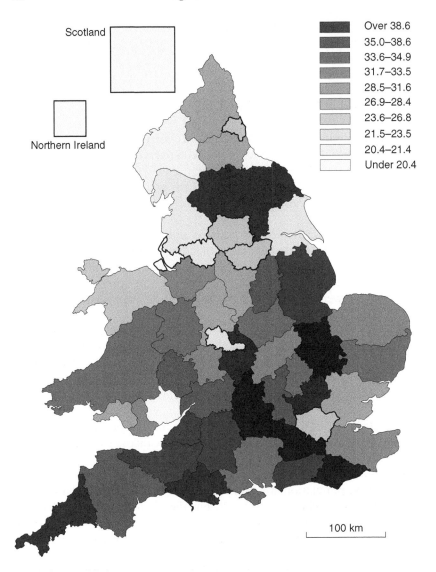

Source: NHSCR.

*Figure 3.3a   UK internal migration: gross in-migration rates per 1000
               population 2009–10*

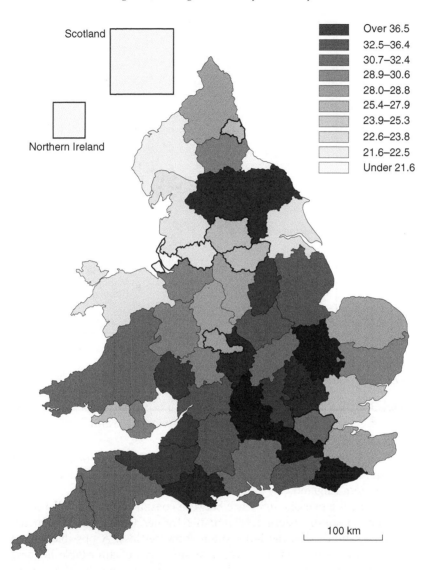

Source: NHSCR.

Figure 3.3b   UK internal migration: gross out-migration rates per 1000
population 2009–10

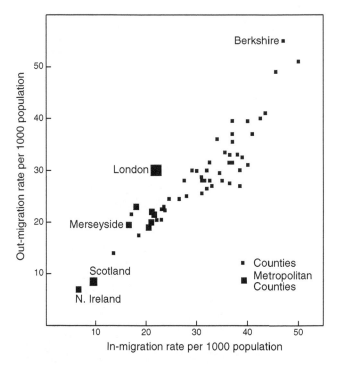

Source: 2001 Census.

Figure 3.4   *UK internal migration 2000–01: the correlation between gross in-migration rates and gross out-migration rates*

on both occasions, especially so the coastal counties of South West England and the counties of Norfolk, Suffolk and Lincolnshire in eastern England.

- There is a marked difference between coastal and non-coastal counties in south-eastern England; the former tend to have high net migration gains, the latter often show net loss. A possible reason for this is that, in the context of shortages of affordable housing consequent upon tight land-use and building controls, those areas that had previously had high elderly populations such as coastal retirement towns have many properties on the market for young adult in-migrant households, whereas those with working-age adult households do not, and that, in addition, the latter tend to lose their student offspring to university cities/counties.

- Major cities in former old industrial regions tend to show net loss; this is true for the large northern cities such as Newcastle, Sheffield,

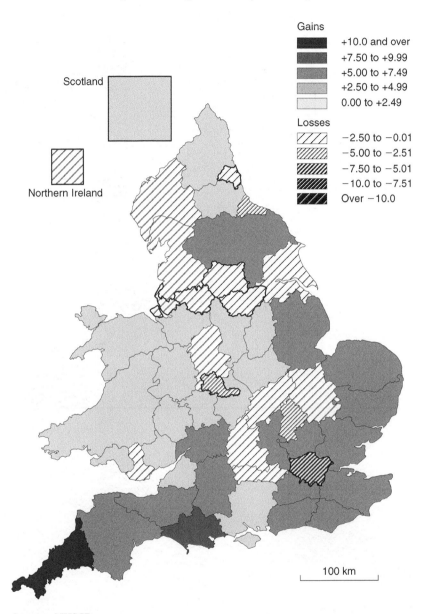

Gains

+10.0 and over
+7.50 to +9.99
+5.00 to +7.49
+2.50 to +4.99
0.00 to +2.49

Losses

−2.50 to −0.01
−5.00 to −2.51
−7.50 to −5.01
−10.0 to −7.51
Over −10.0

Scotland

Northern Ireland

100 km

Source: NHSCR.

Figure 3.5a   UK internal migration 2009–10: net-migration gains and losses – rates per 1000 population

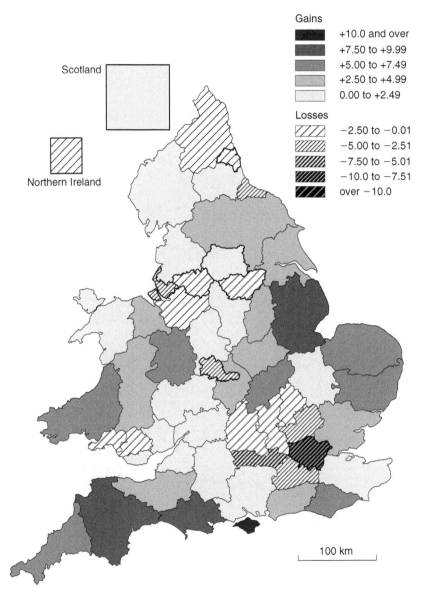

Gains

■	+10.0 and over
■	+7.50 to +9.99
■	+5.00 to +7.49
■	+2.50 to +4.99
▢	0.00 to +2.49

Losses

▨	−2.50 to −0.01
▨	−5.00 to −2.51
▨	−7.50 to −5.01
▨	−10.0 to −7.51
▨	over −10.0

Scotland

Northern Ireland

100 km

Source: 2001 Census.

*Figure 3.5b   UK internal migration 2000–01: net migration rates per 1000
                population*

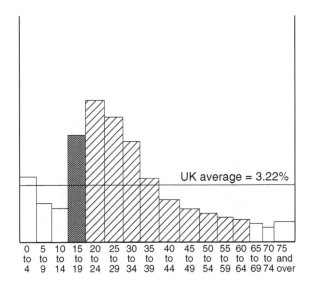

UK average = 3.22%

Source: NHSCR.

Figure 3.6   The age structure of internal migration flows in the United Kingdom in 2009–10. Values relative to UK average

Manchester and Liverpool, but is also true for industrial areas such as Teesside and South Wales.

- Certain scenically attractive areas in northern and western England and Wales show net gains, notably Mid-Wales, Shropshire and North Yorkshire.
- Finally, the rates of loss and gain are rather less in 2009–10 than in 2000–01. This is probably the outcome of the later year being one of recession in the economy (especially affecting the housing market) whereas 2000–01 was a period of growth and economic confidence.

One further general overview picture is provided by Figure 3.6. This simply records the rates of all internal migration flows by five-year age groups, and as might be expected, the peak flows are for people in their 20s, with those aged 15–19 and 30–34 not far behind.

3.4   WALES

The in- and out-migration by age profiles for Wales (Figures 3.7a–c) are interesting and unusual. First, there are clearly two peaks to the inflows:

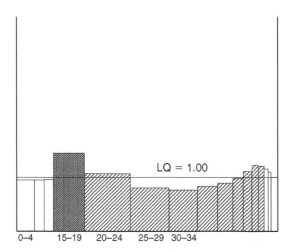

Source: NHSCR.

Location quotients: UK = 1.00

*Figure 3.7a   The age structure of internal migration flows to Wales GOR
from the rest of the UK in 2009–10*

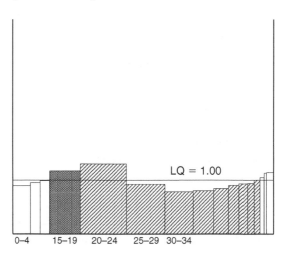

Source: NHSCR.

Location quotients: UK = 1.00

*Figure 3.7b   The age structure of internal migration flows from Wales
GOR to the rest of the UK in 2009–10*

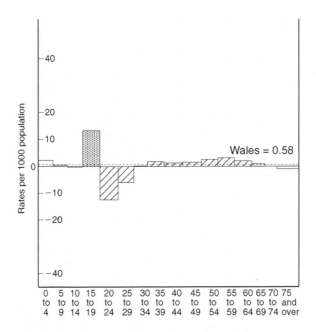

Source: NHSCR.

Figure 3.7c   Net (UK) internal migration by age group for Wales in 2009–10

one of young adults (which is likely to include many students registering at Welsh universities), and the other of older adults in their 50s and 60s (that is, around retirement age). In between these two peaks inflows are distinctively low. The out-migration profile shows many young people leaving Wales, and the peak in the early 20s suggests that many of them are students who are now leaving Wales to take up employment in other regions. Once again, the out-migration rates for mid-career people are low, probably for similar reasons to those suggested for Northern Ireland (a combination of cultural ties and class composition effects). The profile for net migration adds interesting detail to the gross flows. The net loss of young adults is clear, but so also are the small net gains from 35–39 right the way through to retirement age groups with a peak value, not at retirement age, but at 55–59. As we shall see below, Wales (especially rural Wales) figures prominently as a destination for migrants from several English regions.

3.5   NORTH EAST GOR

With employment-related and housing-related migrations falling away
in the economic downturn following the events of autumn 2008, student
migrations have tended to assume a more central role in inter-urban and
inter-regional migration in the UK. The effects of this can be seen in a
rather dramatic form in the case of the North East Government Official
Region (Figures 3.8a–c). The in-migration profile shows a single major
peak in the 15–19 age group and a very minor peak for people in their 50s.
This reflects the attractiveness of the universities in the region, notably
Newcastle and Durham, to students from elsewhere, but mostly from
England and Wales. The out-migration profile confirms this interpretation; the highest rate is for young adults aged 20–24, and the area of the
column above the location quotient of 1.00 is roughly the same as for that
of the area above 1.00 in the in-migration profile. The net migration rates
show that the region was indeed a net gainer of 15–19-year-olds, a net loser
of people in their 20s and early 30s, and that these losses exceeded those
gains to produce an overall slight net loss (–0.75).

It is highly instructive to witness how this overall regional situation is
the product of extremely different migration situations in the four counties
that make up the North East region. The in-, out- and net migration profiles for Tyne and Wear, containing the large formerly primarily industrial
and now university city of Newcastle-upon-Tyne (Figures 3.9a–c), reveal
several interesting details:

● The net gain of 15–19-year-olds is a product of both high in-
  migration and low out-migration.
● Instead of an immediate return of students, there is a more general
  phased out-migration of young adults in their 20s and 30s.
● This then merges with a central city to suburb and peri-urban area
  migration that results in a net loss overall (–1.71), losses of working-
  age adults across all age groups, and of children.

The profiles for Northumberland (Figures 3.10a–c) are, to some extent, a
mirror image of those for Tyne and Wear. This largely rural and coastal
county, which is contiguous with Tyne and Wear has:

● a low in-migration and high out-migration of young people aged
  15–19, producing a very high rate of net loss;
● net gains for almost all working-age groups with returning students
  perhaps adding to the 20–24 age group;
● very sizeable inflows of older adults, resulting in high net gains for

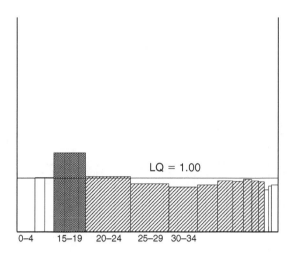

Source: NHSCR.

Location quotients: UK = 1.00

Figure 3.8a   The age structure of internal migration flows to the North East GOR from the rest of the UK in 2009–10

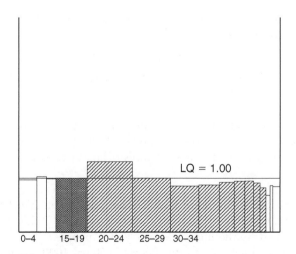

Source: NHSCR.

Location quotients: UK = 1.00

Figure 3.8b   The age structure of internal migration flows from the North East GOR to the rest of the UK in 2009–10

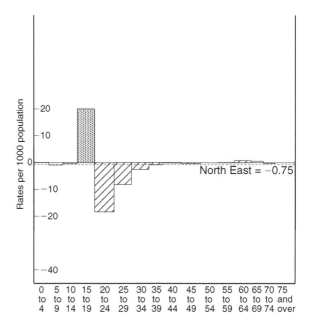

Source: NHSCR.

Figure 3.8c   *Net (UK) internal migration by age group for the North East GOR in 2009–10*

these age groups and contributing to a significant overall net gain (+2.27).

County Durham, like Northumberland, has attractive rural scenery and historic towns and villages, but above all, it has a university. Its in-, out- and net migration profiles (Figures 3.11a–c) reveal a remarkable picture:

- Perhaps due to its more middle-class population, Durham has a larger than average outflow of 15–19-year-olds. But this is massively outweighed by the high inflow of young people in this age group, resulting in a net inflow rate of close to 50 per 1000 population.
- This is almost matched by the net outflow of young adults aged 20–24, with only a small net loss in the 25–29 age group. This is unlike the situation in Tyne and Wear where losses are spread out over several subsequent age groups (probably due to the greater diversity of job opportunities for graduates).

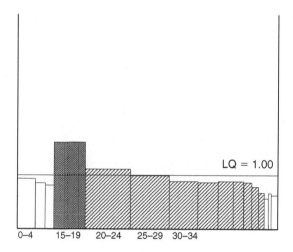

Source: NHSCR.

Location quotients: UK = 1.00

*Figure 3.9a   The age structure of internal migration flows to Tyne and Wear
Metropolitan County (MC) from the rest of the UK in 2009–10*

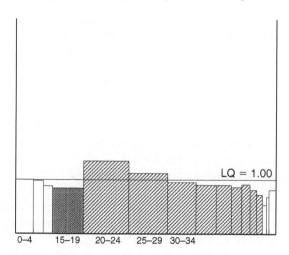

Source: NHSCR.

Location quotients: UK = 1.00

*Figure 3.9b   The age structure of internal migration flows from Tyne and Wear
Metropolitan County (MC) to the rest of the UK in 2009–10*

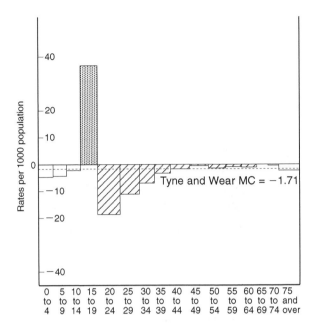

Source: NHSCR.

Figure 3.9c   Net (UK) internal migration by age group for Tyne and Wear Metropolitan County (MC) in 2009–10

- As with Northumberland, Durham then attracts older working-age adults and their children, and some retired people.

But if we map the flows to and from County Durham we can see new features of the university-related internal migration flows. Figures 3.12a and b map the migration velocities for flows to and from County Durham. The inflow map shows a number of distinctive features:

- There are high rates of in-migration from nearby counties, and the Pennine Hills no longer act as a divide as they certainly did in the past (see Fielding, 1971).
- Nevertheless, there is a bias towards higher rates from eastern counties.
- The counties in southern England that send migrants to Durham tend to be those with relatively wealthy, older working-age, middle-class populations (such as Surrey, Berkshire, Oxfordshire, Cambridgeshire and Wiltshire). London, in particular, sends

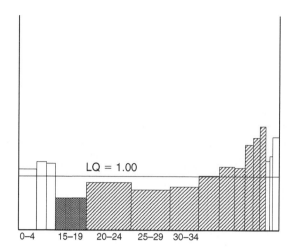

Source: NHSCR.

Location quotients: UK = 1.00

Figure 3.10a   *The age structure of internal migration flows to*
Northumberland from the rest of the UK in 2009–10

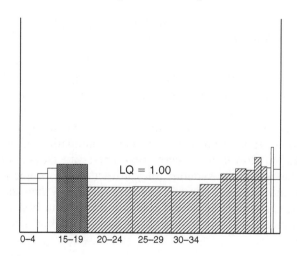

Source: NHSCR.

Location quotients: UK = 1.00

Figure 3.10b   *The age structure of internal migration flows from*
Northumberland to the rest of the UK in 2009–10

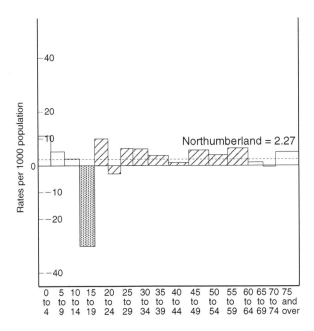

Source: NHSCR.

*Figure 3.10c   Net (UK) internal migration by age group for
Northumberland in 2009–10*

relatively few. The flows from County Durham are similar, except
for two very interesting things: the first is that, true to its university
character, the flows are especially high to the university counties
of Oxford and Cambridge; the second is that the rates of flow to
London are very much higher. This combination of in- and out-
migration flow rates suggest that university cities/counties such
as Durham act as syphons: they attract young people from those
areas most likely to generate university students, then channel them
towards locations in which graduate careers can best be pursued.
That might be other university cities/counties, but, above all, it is
London.

The in-, out- and net migration profiles for Tees (Figures 3.13a–c), an area
that lacks a major university and has a predominantly industrial character, provide a sharp contrast to all of the other profiles for the constituent counties of the North East region. The in-migration profile is slightly
biased towards younger people but otherwise is little different from the

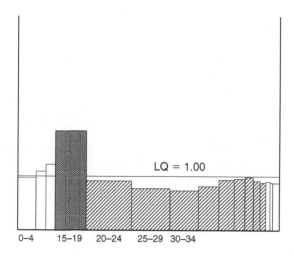

Source: NHSCR.

Location quotients: UK = 1.00

Figure 3.11a *The age structure of internal migration flows to County Durham from the rest of the UK in 2009–10*

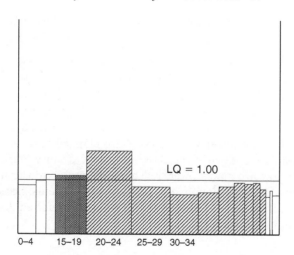

Source: NHSCR.

Location quotients: UK = 1.00

Figure 3.11b *The age structure of internal migration flows from County Durham to the rest of the UK in 2009–10*

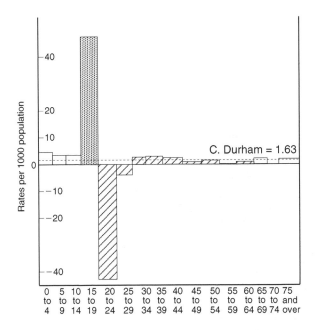

Source: NHSCR.

Figure 3.11c   Net (UK) internal migration by age group for County
            Durham in 2009–10

national picture. The out-migration profile is similar, except that the out-migration rates for young adults are rather high. This then results in a net migration profile that shows losses for the 15–19 age group, and even higher rates of loss for those in their 20s, with a significant overall net loss of –2.37. When the out-migration flows are mapped (Figure 3.14), they look interestingly different from those of nearby County Durham. First, the rates of flow are much lower, reflecting the more industrial working-class nature of the population, and the far fewer students. Second, counties with major university cities do not show up as preferred destinations, but London most certainly does.

3.6   NORTH WEST GOR

The remarkable thing about the North West region's internal migration profiles is how amazingly unremarkable they are. The values for in-, out- and net migration (Figures 3.15a–c) stay very close indeed to the UK

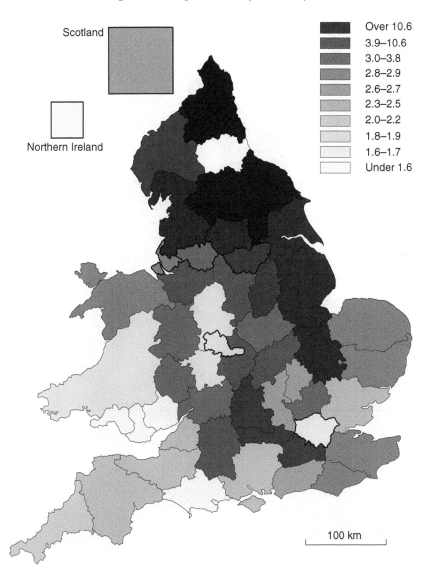

Scotland

Northern Ireland

	Over 10.6
	3.9–10.6
	3.0–3.8
	2.8–2.9
	2.6–2.7
	2.3–2.5
	2.0–2.2
	1.8–1.9
	1.6–1.7
	Under 1.6

100 km

Source: NHSCR.

Figure 3.12a　UK internal migration 2009–10: migration flows to County Durham – migration velocities (see text)

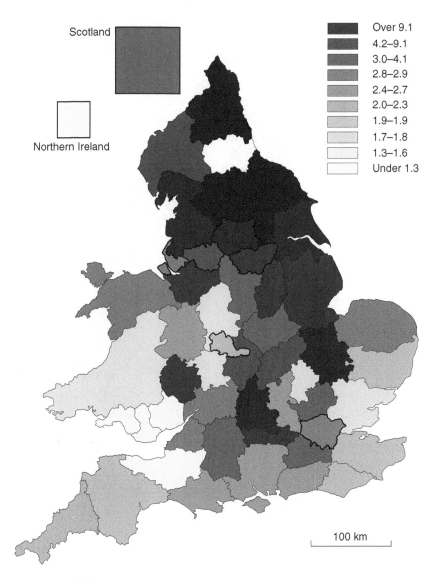

Scotland

Northern Ireland

Over 9.1
4.2–9.1
3.0–4.1
2.8–2.9
2.4–2.7
2.0–2.3
1.9–1.9
1.7–1.8
1.3–1.6
Under 1.3

100 km

Source: NHSCR.

*Figure 3.12b   UK internal migration 2009–10: migration flows from
                County Durham – migration velocities (see text)*

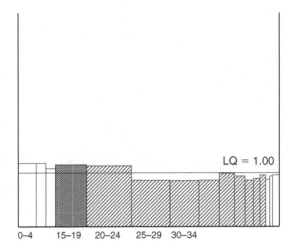

Source: NHSCR.

Location quotients: UK = 1.00

Figure 3.13a   *The age structure of internal migration flows to Tees from the rest of the UK in 2009–10*

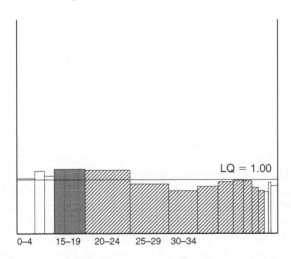

Source: NHSCR.

Location quotients: UK = 1.00

Figure 3.13b   *The age structure of internal migration flows from Tees to the rest of the UK in 2009–10*

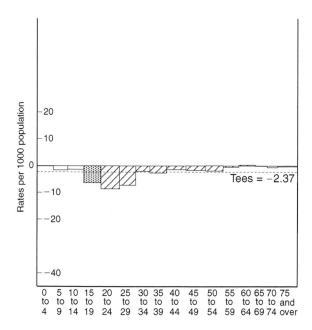

Source: NHSCR.

*Figure 3.13c   Net (UK) internal migration by age group for Tees in
              2009–10*

averages over all age groups; the only minor exception is the fact that the
region loses population through net internal migration (–1.04) and that
the rates of loss are slightly higher for young adults in their 20s than for
other age groups.

When one looks at the patterns below the level of the region, however,
distinctive features emerge. Merseyside Metropolitan County, containing
the industrial, port and university city of Liverpool has been chosen for
closer inspection. The profiles are shown in Figures 3.16a–c. These show
first that there is a modest gain of 15–19-year-olds as a result of both a
higher rate of in-migration and a slightly lower rate of out-migration; and
second, that, like Newcastle, the net gain of young people was more than
matched by the net out-migration of young adults in their 20s and 30s,
only some of whom were students graduating and moving on to employment elsewhere, resulting in a net overall loss of –1.60.

Merseyside, however, illustrates another point rather well. Northern
former major industrial conurbations tend to have low overall rates of
in-migration and out-migration and their migration fields tend to be local

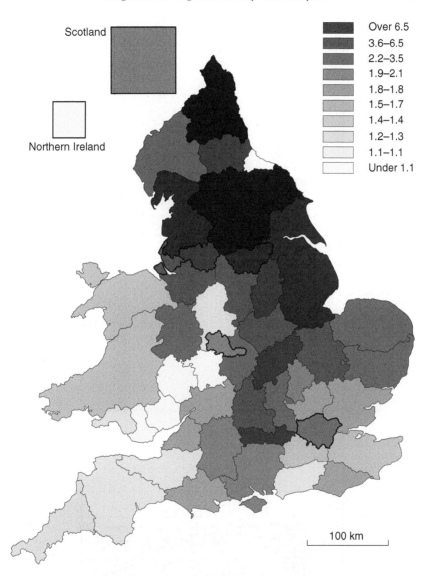

Source: NHSCR.

*Figure 3.14   UK internal migration 2009–10: migration flows from Tees –
migration velocities (see text)*

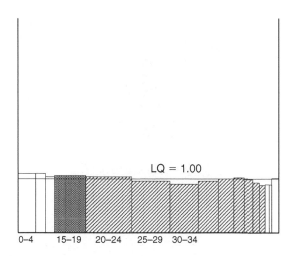

Source: NHSCR.

Location quotients: UK = 1.00

*Figure 3.15a   The age structure of internal migration flows to the North
                 West GOR from the rest of the UK in 2009–10*

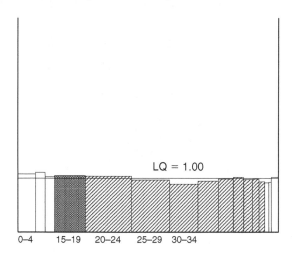

Source: NHSCR.

Location quotients: UK = 1.00

*Figure 3.15b   The age structure of internal migration flows from the North
                 West GOR to the rest of the UK in 2009–10*

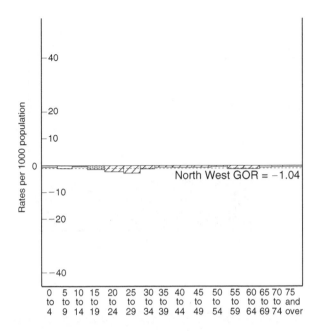

Source: NHSCR.

*Figure 3.15c Net (UK) internal migration by age group for North West
GOR in 2009–10*

rather than regional or national. This can be shown by a comparison
between Merseyside and Berkshire (in the South East GOR). In Figures
3.17a and b, the convention used elsewhere of mapping the migration
velocities by decile is abandoned in favour of common and equal-inter-
val categories. This has the advantage that the out-migration fields of
Merseyside and Berkshire can be directly compared. The outcome is pre-
dictable, but nevertheless striking. The Merseyside migration field is much
smaller geographically and the migration velocities are lower.

3.7 YORKSHIRE & HUMBER GOR

Like the North East, the Yorkshire & Humber region is a formerly heavily
industrialized region that now has a number of large universities located in
its major cities (notably Leeds, Bradford, Sheffield, York and Hull). So its
in-, out- and net migration profiles (Figures 3.18a–c) are not dissimilar to
those for the North East. The in-migration of 15–19-year-olds dominates

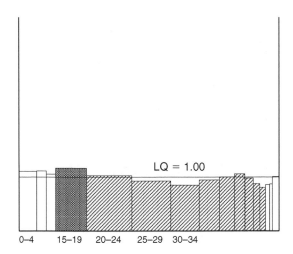

Source: NHSCR.

Location quotients: UK = 1.00

Figure 3.16a   *The age structure of internal migration flows to Merseyside from the rest of the UK in 2009–10*

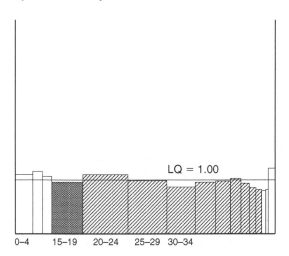

Source: NHSCR.

Location quotients: UK = 1.00

Figure 3.16b   *The age structure of internal migration flows from Merseyside to the rest of the UK in 2009–10*

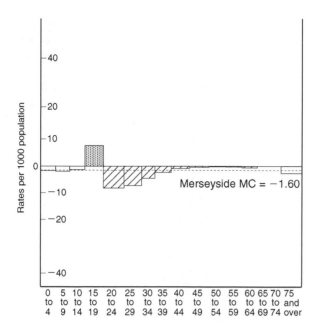

Source: NHSCR.

Figure 3.16c   Net (UK) internal migration by age group for Merseyside Metropolitan County (MC) in 2009–10

the inflow, and the out-migration of 20–24-year-olds dominates the outflow. The net migration profile shows both the net gains of the former and the net losses of the latter, but it also shows the further net losses of working-age adults to produce a small overall net loss of –1.14.

In Figures 3.19a–c we focus on a level below that of the county, in fact on just one university city: Sheffield. This former steel and metal goods industrial city now has a surprisingly youthful population, and its migration profiles are very distinctive. Net loss characterizes every age group except just one: the 15–19 age group. The annual in-migration rate for this group amounts to a remarkable 12 per cent of the population in that age group in Sheffield.

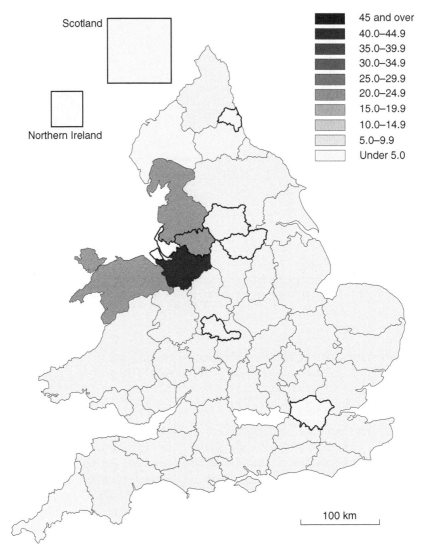

Scotland

Northern Ireland

45 and over
40.0–44.9
35.0–39.9
30.0–34.9
25.0–29.9
20.0–24.9
15.0–19.9
10.0–14.9
5.0–9.9
Under 5.0

100 km

Source: NHSCR.

*Figure 3.17a   UK internal migration 2009–10: migration flows from
Merseyside Metropolitan County (MC) – migration
velocities (see text)*

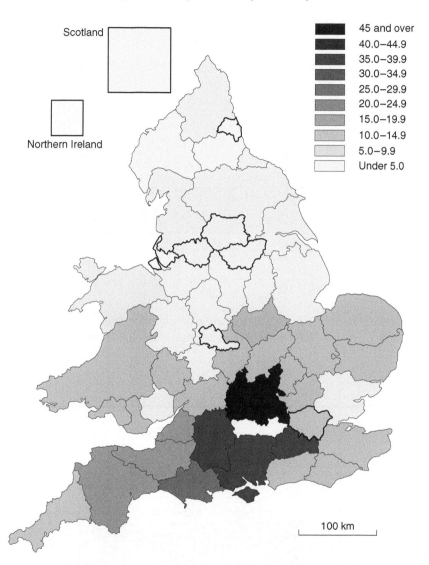

Source: NHSCR.

Figure 3.17b UK internal migration 2009–10: migration flows from
Berkshire – migration velocities (see text)

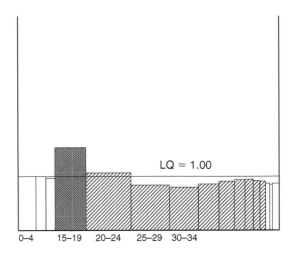

Source:	NHSCR.

Location quotients: UK = 1.00

*Figure 3.18a	The age structure of internal migration flows to the Yorkshire
& Humber GOR from the rest of the UK in 2009–10*

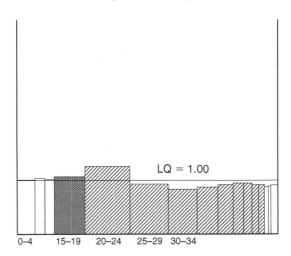

Source:	NHSCR.

Location quotients: UK = 1.00

*Figure 3.18b	The age structure of internal migration flows from the
Yorkshire & Humber GOR to the rest of the UK in 2009–10*

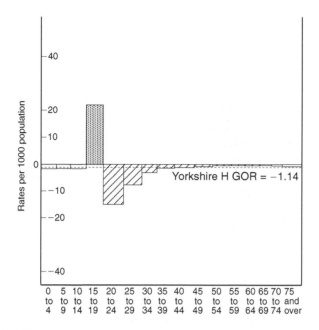

Source: NHSCR.

*Figure 3.18c   Net (UK) internal migration by age group for Yorkshire
              & Humber GOR in 2009–10*

3.8   EAST MIDLANDS GOR

Once again, the East Midlands is a region with cities containing large
universities (notably Nottingham and Leicester), but this time, instead of
the region having a history of manufacturing industry decline, it is one
of recent manufacturing and service industry growth. This means that,
although the in-, out- and net migration profiles (Figures 3.20a–c) resemble those of Yorkshire & Humber, the net gains over the middle and later
working-age groups ensure a small overall net migration gain of +1.38.
Particularly interesting is that the out-migration profile shows high rates
of loss in the 15–19 age group, so it seems that many students leave to
study and train in other regions, albeit outnumbered by the many from
outside who migrate to the East Midlands to study.

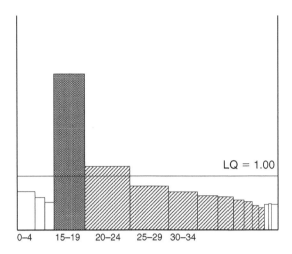

Source: NHSCR.

Location quotients: UK = 1.00

*Figure 3.19a   The age structure of internal migration flows to Sheffield
from the rest of the UK in 2009–10*

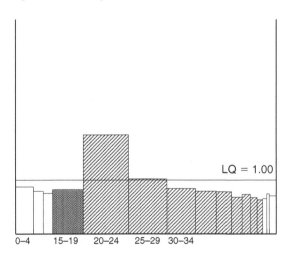

Source: NHSCR.

Location quotients: UK = 1.00

*Figure 3.19b   The age structure of internal migration flows from Sheffield
to the rest of the UK in 2009–10*

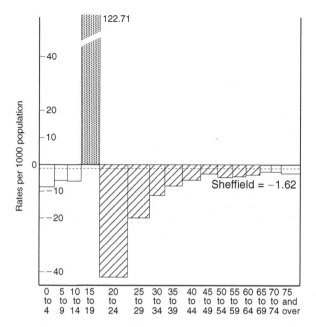

Source: NHSCR.

Figure 3.19c   *Net (UK) internal migration by age group for Sheffield in 2009–10*

3.9 WEST MIDLANDS GOR

The migration-by-age profiles for the West Midlands region are very similar indeed to those for the North West. This means that in-, out- and net migration rates (see Figures 3.21a–c) closely resemble those for the country as a whole. The only difference is that the West Midlands economy has performed rather poorly in the recent period; it can be seen that an overall loss of –1.75 has resulted, in particular, from the net losses of young people and young adults.

Once again, within the West Midlands region there is significant variation. This time, instead of focusing on a university county/city, we examine the profiles for Shropshire, a relatively rural county without a university. This county is located between urban-industrial West Midlands and rural Mid-Wales, to the west of both Birmingham and its surrounding West Midlands Metropolitan County, and of the industrial areas of Staffordshire. Its in-, out- and net migration profiles are shown

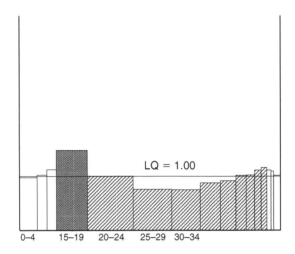

Source: NHSCR.

Location quotients: UK = 1.00

*Figure 3.20a   The age structure of internal migration flows to the East
                 Midlands GOR from the rest of the UK in 2009–10*

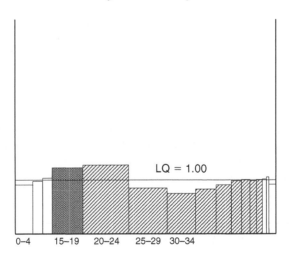

Source: NHSCR.

Location quotients: UK = 1.00

*Figure 3.20b   The age structure of internal migration flows from the East
                 Midlands GOR to the rest of the UK in 2009–10*

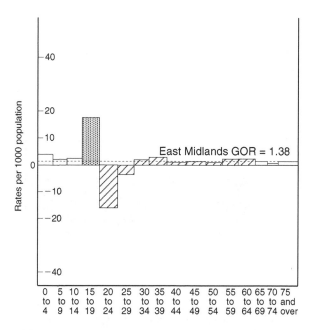

Source: NHSCR.

Figure 3.20c   Net (UK) internal migration by age group for the East Midlands GOR in 2009–10

in Figures 3.22a–c. The in-migration rates are high for people aged over 40 years old, and for older children, indicating, since employment opportunities are limited, that these are either long-distance commuters, or people of independent means, or retirees. The out-migration rates are especially high for young people aged 15–19, suggesting that they are leaving Shropshire to work, study and train elsewhere. The net migration profile confirms what has been presented above; although an overall net gainer by internal migration (+1.26), Shropshire is a massive loser of young people and young adults with little sign of a compensating return of graduates in the 20–24 age group.

3.10   EAST GOR

The migration profiles for this region (Figures 3.23a–c) are almost a mirror image of those for a northern formerly industrial university city such as Sheffield or Newcastle. The in-migration profile is biased towards

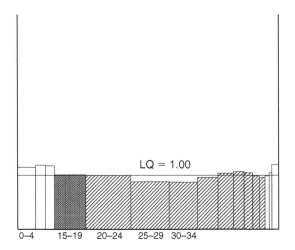

Source: NHSCR.

Location quotients: UK = 1.00

Figure 3.21a   *The age structure of internal migration flows to the West*
                  Midlands GOR from the rest of the UK in 2009–10

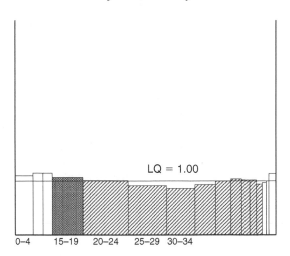

Source: NHSCR.

Location quotients: UK = 1.00

Figure 3.21b   *The age structure of internal migration flows from the West*
                  Midlands GOR to the rest of the UK in 2009–10

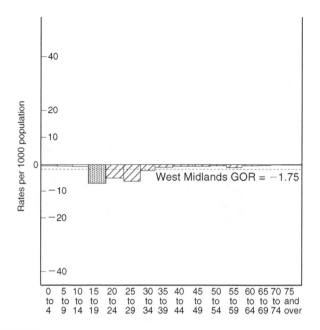

Source: NHSCR.

Figure 3.21c   Net (UK) internal migration by age group for the West Midlands GOR in 2009–10

older people both in, and beyond, the official working-age groups. Despite the presence of large universities such as those in Cambridge, Norwich and Colchester, there is a distinct lack of in-migrants in the 15–19 age group. Instead, as is shown by the out-migration profile, the region loses many of its 15–19-year-olds. The net migration rates confirm this; indeed, it is the only age group to lose through migration; all the rest experience migration gains and these gains are spread fairly evenly across the age groups, resulting in a significant overall net gain (+2.26) for the region.

Norfolk rather effectively illustrates the situation. It is a fairly rural county with historic towns and a long coastline. It has a university. The migration profiles (Figures 3.24a–c) show that:

- Norfolk is attractive to people in the older working-age groups, and to the retired;
- it also attracts people in their 30s and 40s along with their children;
- despite the presence of the university, it loses young people and young adults.

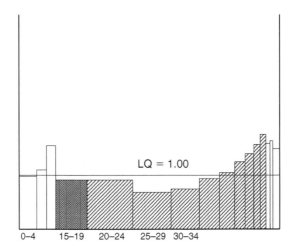

Source: NHSCR.

Location quotients: UK = 1.00

Figure 3.22a   *The age structure of internal migration flows to Shropshire from the rest of the UK in 2009–10*

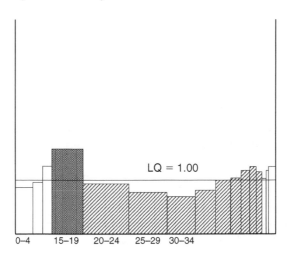

Source: NHSCR.

Location quotients: UK = 1.00

Figure 3.22b   *The age structure of internal migration flows from Shropshire to the rest of the UK in 2009–10*

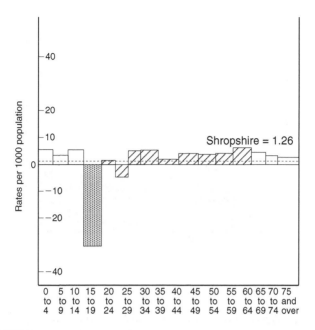

Source: NHSCR.

Figure 3.22c   Net (UK) internal migration by age group for Shropshire in 2009–10

3.11 LONDON

London is an amazing city in all sorts of ways, including, as it turns out, its unique relations to the rest of the UK through internal migration flows. These profiles are shown in Figures 3.25a–c. This uniqueness derives from:

- the massive concentration of both in-migration rates and out-migration rates in the working-age groups;
- the extraordinarily low in-migration of older adults and the retired;
- the combination of very low in-migration and very low out-migration for young people aged 15–19;
- the fact that it is the only major city in the UK that has a net loss of 15–19-year-olds; and
- the fact that, despite its very high rate of overall net loss (−5.26), it has significant migration gains of people in their 20s, especially those aged 20–24.

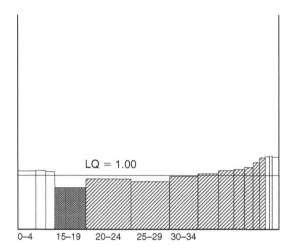

Source: NHSCR.

Location quotients: UK = 1.00

Figure 3.23a   *The age structure of internal migration flows to the East*
                  GOR from the rest of the UK in 2009–10

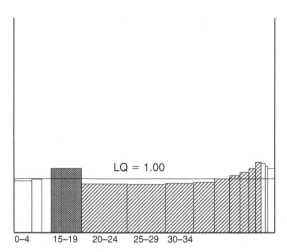

Source: NHSCR.

Location quotients: UK = 1.00

Figure 3.23b   *The age structure of internal migration flows from the East*
                  GOR to the rest of the UK in 2009–10

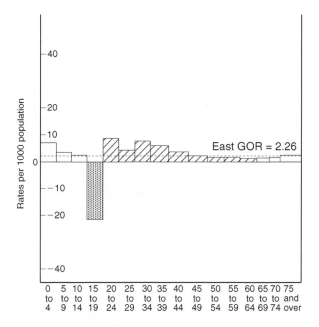

Source: NHSCR.

Figure 3.23c Net (UK) internal migration by age group for the East GOR in 2009–10

Other noteworthy features of the distributions are the following:

- The peak for in-migration rates is to the left (that is, younger) than the peak for out-migration rates.
- The out-migration rate for young adults aged 20–24 is particularly low.
- The rates of net loss are almost equally high for all ages other than those in their 20s; thus London loses by internal migration many children, young people at school-leaving and university entrance years, people in their 30s, 40s, 50s, 60s, and beyond. It is a truly remarkable picture.

Remarkable it may be, but if we look at the profiles for Inner London, specifically Camden and Islington (Figures 3.26a–c), we can see the same features in an even more extreme form, with even higher rates of gain in the young adult age groups and even higher rates of loss for all the other age groups – with one glaring exception. The 15–19 age group switches

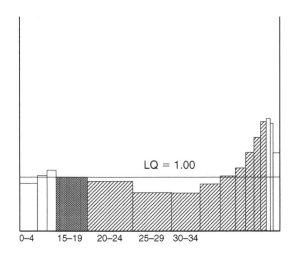

Source: NHSCR.

Location quotients: UK = 1.00

*Figure 3.24a   The age structure of internal migration flows to Norfolk
              from the rest of the UK in 2009–10*

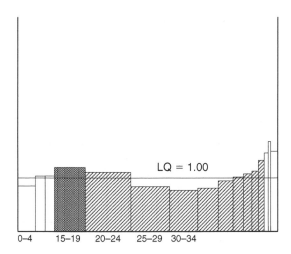

Source: NHSCR.

Location quotients: UK = 1.00

*Figure 3.24b   The age structure of internal migration flows from Norfolk
              to the rest of the UK in 2009–10*

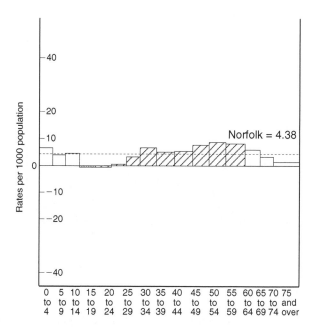

Source: NHSCR.

Figure 3.24c   Net (UK) internal migration by age group for Norfolk in 2009–10

from being net loss for London overall, to being an extraordinary net gain for these two Inner London boroughs (explained in large part by the fact that Camden and Islington are the nearest student residential areas to the main campuses of the University of London). But Figure 3.26c also shows how extremely youthful the population of Inner London has become; notice the great width of the columns for those in their 20s and 30s. And yet the high rate of loss for the under 5s is also noteworthy; Inner London is, for many of those young adults who are in a position to choose, a place to be avoided when raising a family.

So what is the geography of the migration flows that results in London's unique profiles? Figures 3.27a and b show the in-migration flows and out-migration flows expressed in migration velocities, while Figure 3.27c shows the net flows to London. A number of features stand out in these maps:

- The highest rates of flow to London tend to be south and east of a line drawn from the Severn to the Wash.

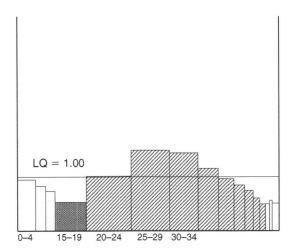

Source: NHSCR.

Location quotients: UK = 1.00

Figure 3.25a   *The age structure of internal migration flows to London*
                  GOR from the rest of the UK in 2009–10

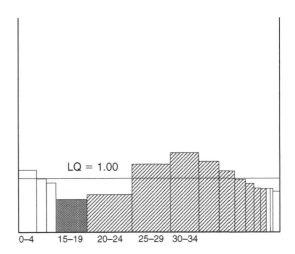

Source: NHSCR.

Location quotients: UK = 1.00

Figure 3.25b   *The age structure of internal migration flows from London*
                  GOR to the rest of the UK in 2009–10

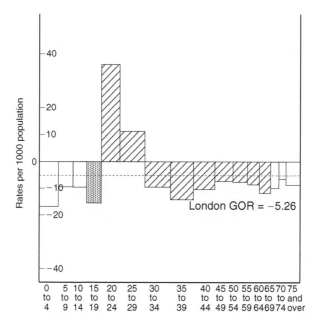

Source: NHSCR.

Figure 3.25c   *Net (UK) internal migration by age group for the London GOR in 2009–10*

- However, when areas to the north and west of this have high values, they tend to be the largest cities and cities with large universities (Birmingham, Leeds, Manchester, Newcastle, Nottingham and Cardiff).
- The highest rates of flow from London tend to be to the same areas south and east of the Severn/Wash line.
- Areas to the north and west of this line tend to have values that are lower than for in-migration.
- Not surprisingly, therefore, the net flows show mostly gains to London from the north and west, and losses from London to the south and east.
- The exceptions to this rule are fascinating – the net losses from London in the north and west are mostly rural (Mid-Wales, Lincolnshire, Herefordshire and Northumberland), while the areas south and east of the line that are net gainers to London are the counties containing the three university cities of Oxford, Cambridge and Bristol (remember the comments earlier about the role of university cities as

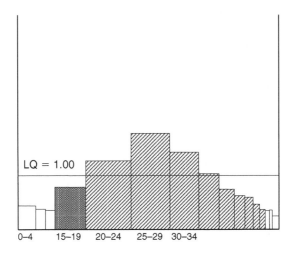

Source: NHSCR.

Location quotients: UK = 1.00

Figure 3.26a   The age structure of internal migration flows to Camden and Islington from the rest of the UK in 2009–10

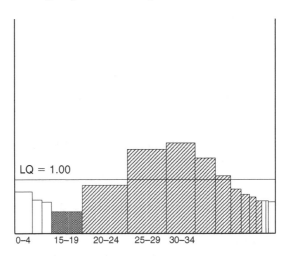

Source: NHSCR.

Location quotients: UK = 1.00

Figure 3.26b   The age structure of internal migration flows from Camden and Islington to the rest of the UK in 2009–10

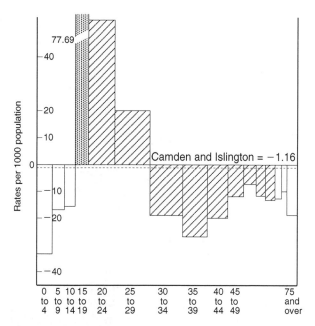

Source: NHSCR.

Figure 3.26c   Net (UK) internal migration by age group for Camden and Islington in 2009–10

syphons – collecting young people from many, mainly middle-class counties, and then channelling them towards London).

The in-migration and out-migration flows using migration velocities were also mapped for 2000–01 (not shown here). The differences from 2009–10 are quite small and yet very interesting. For the in-migration flows the rates were, on average slightly lower in 2000–01 than in 2009–10, but in the latter year, the flows to London from the large university cities of the Midlands and North (Birmingham, Nottingham, Sheffield, Leeds, Manchester and Liverpool) were markedly higher, indicating possibly the increased importance of student migrations in the system. The out-migration flows from London were significantly higher in 2000–01 than in 2009–10, which is what might be expected given the fact that the earlier date was a year of buoyant labour and housing markets, when both firms and individuals tended to invest outside the metropolitan region. The patterns of outflow are, however, very similar; there is just a slight tendency for the flows in the earlier period to be more biased towards rural areas than in 2009–10.

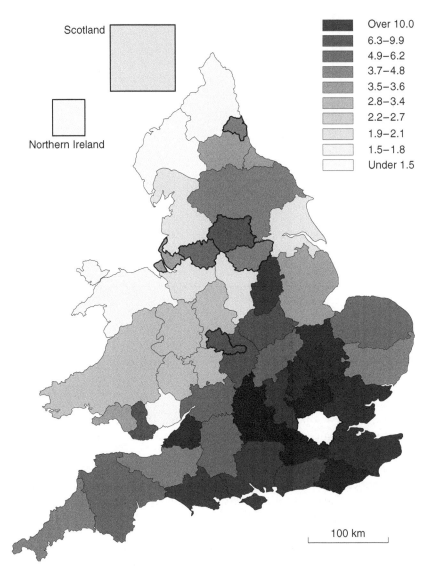

Source: NHSCR.

*Figure 3.27a   UK internal migration 2009–10: migration flows to London
            – migration velocities (see text)*

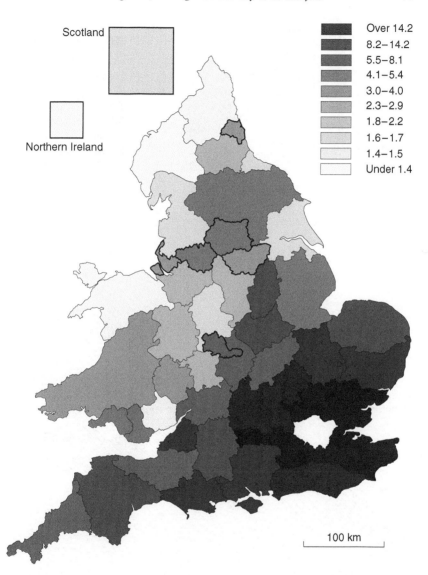

Scotland

Northern Ireland

	Over 14.2
	8.2−14.2
	5.5−8.1
	4.1−5.4
	3.0−4.0
	2.3−2.9
	1.8−2.2
	1.6−1.7
	1.4−1.5
	Under 1.4

100 km

Source: NHSCR.

*Figure 3.27b   UK internal migration 2009–10: migration flows from
London – migration velocities (see text)*

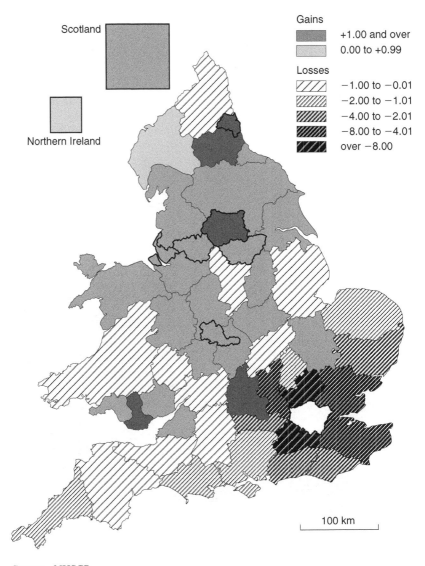

Gains

■ +1.00 and over
░ 0.00 to +0.99

Losses

▨ −1.00 to −0.01
▨ −2.00 to −1.01
▨ −4.00 to −2.01
▨ −8.00 to −4.01
▨ over −8.00

Scotland

Northern Ireland

100 km

Source: NHSCR.

*Figure 3.27c   UK internal migration 2009–10: net migration gains and
losses to London – migration velocities (see text)*

3.12 SOUTH EAST GOR

It is obvious to all who use official regional statistics in the UK that the 'London' region does not coincide with the functional city-region of the capital. That functional city-region stretches way out into the South East GOR and into the East GOR. So, when we inspect the age profiles of migration into and away from the South East GOR we should expect features that reflect the suburban and peri-urban ties that these areas have with London.

This suburban, peri-urban, 'Home Counties' feature of the South East GOR is rather clearly demonstrated by the region's age-specific in- and out- and net migration rates (Figures 3.28a–c). The in-migration rate profile shows that the region is attractive to middle and older working-age adults (and their teenage children), and to the retired. Younger adults have lower than average rates of in-migration; they would probably find it difficult to afford the housing in the South East. The house prices here are kept high by severe shortages, which are made worse by the NIMBY ('not in my back yard') behaviours of a majority of the current middle-class residents, who are usually extremely effective at mobilizing against further house building. The 15–19 age group is interesting (location quotients = approximately 1.00). Undoubtedly some of these in-migrants are older children accompanying their parents, but it is also the case that this region has some large universities located within it (notably Oxford, Reading, Southampton and Sussex). Normally, the in- and out-migration rates for the 15–19 age group compensate one another, so that if one is above the average, the other is below. But the out-migration profile shows a much higher than average rate of out-migration for the 15–19 age group; this is probably because the relatively wealthy inhabitants produce a higher than average number of university students, many of whom leave the region to study elsewhere. The picture is completed by the net migration profile. Overall, the region is characterized by significant net gain. But two age groups do not conform: the first consists of young people, many of whom will be attending universities in the major cities of the Midlands and North; the second consists of people in the older working-age groups and the 'young old'.

These two features of the net migration profile are shown much more vividly in the case of Buckinghamshire (Figures 3.29a–c). With no significant university, it has few in-migrants and very many out-migrants in the 15–19 age group. It then gains migrants in the 20–24 age group, presumably many of them graduates returning from their university cities, gains young and middle-aged working adults (many of them probably commuters to jobs in London), then loses older working-age people (a

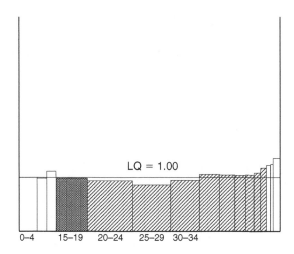

Source: NHSCR.

Location quotients: UK = 1.00

*Figure 3.28a   The age structure of internal migration flows to the South
              East GOR from the rest of the UK in 2009–10*

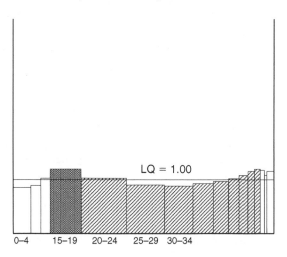

Source: NHSCR.

Location quotients: UK = 1.00

*Figure 3.28b   The age structure of internal migration flows from the South
              East GOR to the rest of the UK in 2009–10*

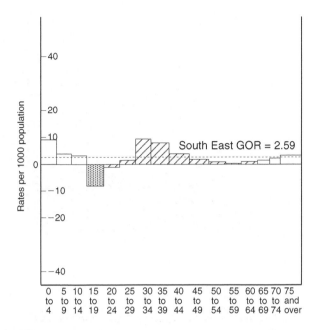

Source: NHSCR.

Figure 3.28c   Net (UK) internal migration by age group for the South East GOR in 2009–10

proportion of them likely to be taking early retirement). Standing back from the detail, and anticipating results yet to be discussed for Wiltshire and Cornwall, it is possible to see a clear pattern of links between these profiles. London, especially Inner London, attracts many upwardly mobile young adults (Champion and Coombs, 2010); some of these are sufficiently successful to move to the expensive semi-rural 'Home Counties' such as Buckinghamshire where they raise their families. The young people from these households are then very likely to out-migrate by going to universities outside London and the South East; the valuable housing assets of these now 'empty nest' parental households are then used to (often more than) finance a move, sometimes before official retirement age, even further away from London, especially towards the South West Peninsula (Dorset, Devon and Cornwall), but also towards the Cotswolds, or rural Wales.

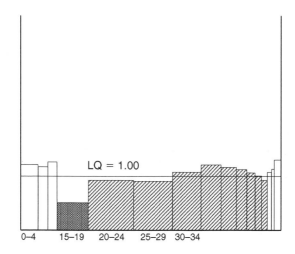

Source: NHSCR.

Location quotients: UK = 1.00

*Figure 3.29a   The age structure of internal migration flows to
                 Buckinghamshire from the rest of the UK in 2009–10*

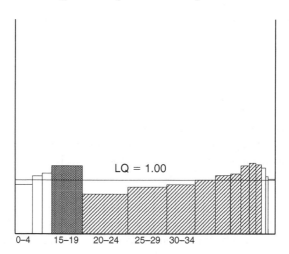

Source: NHSCR.

Location quotients: UK = 1.00

*Figure 3.29b   The age structure of internal migration flows from
                 Buckinghamshire to the rest of the UK in 2009–10*

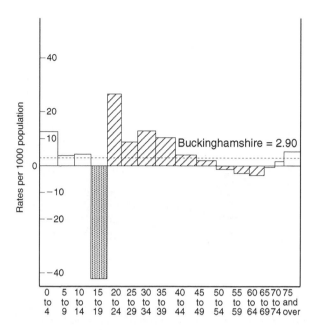

Source: NHSCR.

Figure 3.29c Net (UK) internal migration by age group for Buckinghamshire in 2009–10

3.13 SOUTH WEST GOR

And so to the final region – and what an interesting region for migration flows it turns out to be! The in-, out- and net migration age profiles are shown in Figures 3.30a–c. The in-migration profile is almost a mirror image of that of London, except that the young adults who do not go to the South West region are rather older than the young adults who do go to London. The combination of older working-age adults bringing their teenage children with them, and the attractiveness of the South West to university students (there are major universities at several cities in the region, notably Bristol and Exeter) results in a higher than average in-migration of 15–19-year-olds. But even more striking is the in-migration of those in their 40s, 50s, and above all, their 60s. The region is clearly sought after by those in the pre-retirement, early retirement and retirement age groups.

The out-migration profile also shows higher than average values for the older working-age and retirement populations, but the really distinctive

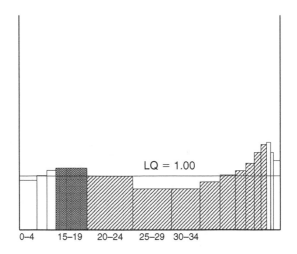

Source: NHSCR.

Location quotients: UK = 1.00

*Figure 3.30a   The age structure of internal migration flows to the South
            West GOR from the rest of the UK in 2009–10*

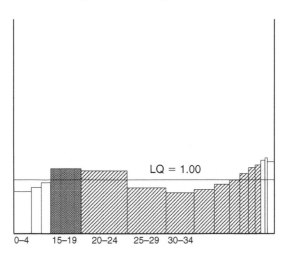

Source: NHSCR.

Location quotients: UK = 1.00

*Figure 3.30b   The age structure of internal migration flows from the South
            West GOR to the rest of the UK in 2009–10*

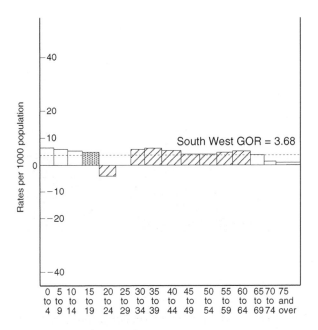

Source: NHSCR.

Figure 3.30c   Net (UK) internal migration by age group for the South West GOR in 2009–10

feature of this profile is the high rates of out-migration of those aged between 15 and 24. This outflow is likely to consist of three elements:

- young people deciding to leave the region to look for employment opportunities elsewhere;
- young people leaving the region to take up university places elsewhere; and
- graduates from universities in the region seeking employment elsewhere (and from what we have seen before, many of these will be migrating to London).

The net migration profile shows overall a large gain for the South West region, and it shows also that the net gain is across all age groups except young adults. This again, is a mirror image of the profile of net gains and losses for London.

As a relatively affluent, largely rural county without a university, Wiltshire's age-specific migration flows (Figures 3.31a–c) show the now

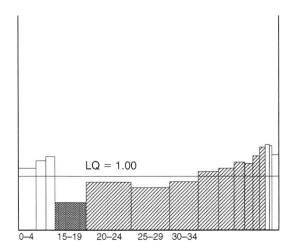

Source: NHSCR.

Location quotients: UK = 1.00

*Figure 3.31a   The age structure of internal migration flows to Wiltshire
from the rest of the UK in 2009–10*

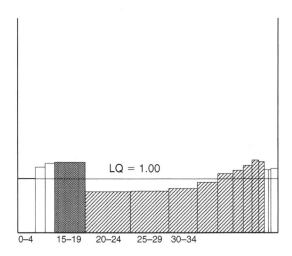

Source: NHSCR.

Location quotients: UK = 1.00

*Figure 3.31b   The age structure of internal migration flows from Wiltshire
to the rest of the UK in 2009–10*

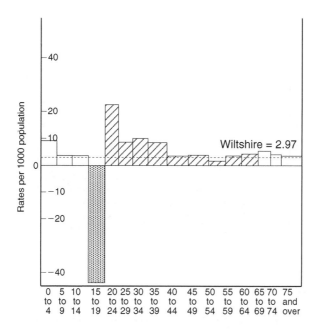

Source: NHSCR.

Figure 3.31c *Net (UK) internal migration by age group for Wiltshire in 2009–10*

familiar marked lack of in-migrants and big excess of out-migrants in the 15–19 age group. The attractiveness of the county to the older working-age and retirement age populations is also clear. What is interesting in the net migration profile is the significant degree to which there is a 'bounce back' from the loss of the 15–19-year-olds. This rather suggests that there are sufficient employment opportunities in the county to attract those who have recently graduated, some, perhaps many, of whom were brought up and left school in the county. As can be seen below for Cornwall, this is by no means always the case.

Cornwall and the Isles of Scilly represents a kind of extreme example of the South West region's dominant migration characteristics. Its reputation as a high-amenity area (based on fine coastal scenery, favourable climate and historic towns and villages) has helped to produce not only a massive overall gain by internal migration (+7.52) but also unusually high in-migration rates for those in their 50s, 60s and 70s (see Figures 3.32a–c below). It is highly significant that the only age group to experience net migration loss is the 15–19 age group. But notice that the rates of gain for

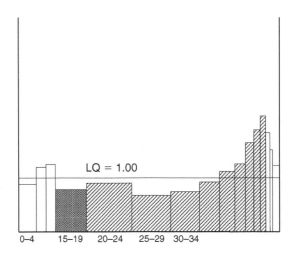

Source: NHSCR.

Location quotients: UK = 1.00

Figure 3.32a   *The age structure of internal migration flows to Cornwall*
and Isles of Scilly from the rest of the UK in 2009–10

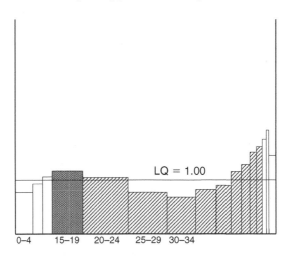

Source: NHSCR.

Location quotients: UK = 1.00

Figure 3.32b   *The age structure of internal migration flows from Cornwall*
and Isles of Scilly to the rest of the UK in 2009–10

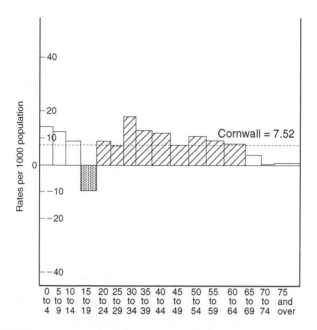

Source: NHSCR.

Figure 3.32c   Net (UK) internal migration by age group for Cornwall in 2009–10

those in retirement age groups are very modest. Cornwall attracts, above all, those in the pre-retirement age groups. Almost as many older people leave (probably in many cases to become close to family members living in south-east England, and presumably sometimes after the death of a spouse), as arrive in the county. The maps of flows to and from Cornwall (Figures 3.33a and b) confirm much of what has been suggested above. Those migrating to Cornwall come from all over England, but especially from the South West region and from counties around and to the west of London (notice, however, not so many from London itself). Those migrating from Cornwall show a similar pattern, but with a strong bias towards rural areas (notice, for example, the high values for Mid-Wales and Norfolk). The net migration map (Figure 3.33c) is especially interesting (note that this is for 2000–01). Those young people leaving Cornwall probably contribute greatly to the net gains for Devon (after all, Plymouth is just across the border and is the nearest high-order service centre for the population of Cornwall), and counties containing university cities such as Exeter, Bristol, Cardiff and Swansea also receive more migrants from

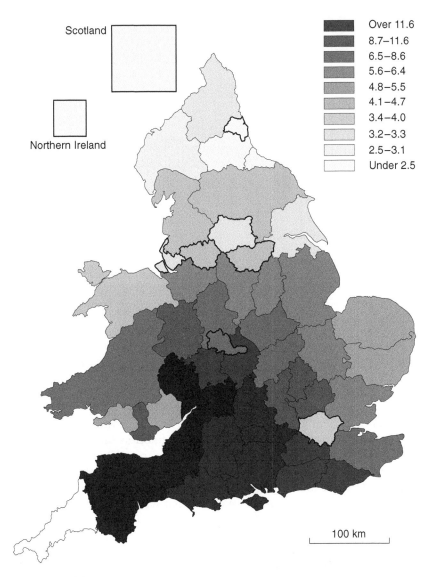

Source: NHSCR.

*Figure 3.33a   UK internal migration 2009–10: migration flows to
            Cornwall – migration velocities (see text)*

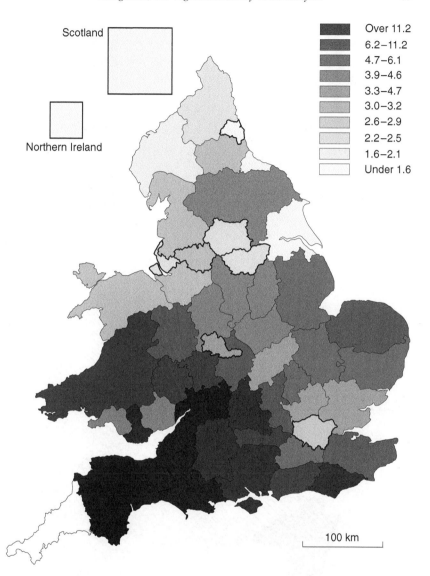

Scotland

Northern Ireland

	Over 11.2
	6.2–11.2
	4.7–6.1
	3.9–4.6
	3.3–4.7
	3.0–3.2
	2.6–2.9
	2.2–2.5
	1.6–2.1
	Under 1.6

100 km

Source: NHSCR.

*Figure 3.33b   UK internal migration 2009–10: migration flows from
            Cornwall – migration velocities (see text)*

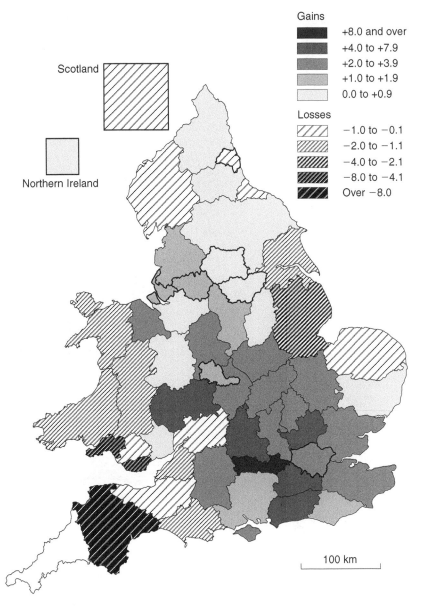

2001 Census SMS.

Figure 3.33c *UK internal migration 2000–01: net migration gains and*
losses to Cornwall and Isles of Scilly – migration velocities
(see text)

Cornwall than they send. But the dominant feature of this final map is the zone of high rates of net gain to Cornwall from the counties of South East England, notably the 'Home Counties' around and to the west of London, with a similar but smaller feature around Birmingham. This conforms well with the notion of a two-stage internal migration pattern away from the metropolitan cities; the first towards suburban and peri-urban counties, and the second towards the UK periphery (northern and western Scotland, northern, central and south-west Wales, and, of course, Devon and Cornwall).

3.14 CONCLUDING REMARKS

This section has described in considerable detail some of the important features of the internal migration flows in the United Kingdom at both regional/country and county levels for both the recent period (2009–10) and at the time of the last population Census (2000–01). Amongst many things it has shown the following:

1. The in- and out-migration rates for certain regions and counties are extraordinarily low while others are just as surprisingly high. The reasons for the low rates must surely include geographical remoteness, the strength of cultural identity, and population size, but in addition, as will be shown below, the social class composition of the population seems to be absolutely crucial to an understanding of differences across counties in in- and out-migration rates. The fact that the gross in- and out-migration rates are strongly positively correlated (when economic logic suggests that they should be negatively related) represents a challenge to our understanding and must be confronted in the next part of this account.
2. London plays a central role in the UK migration system. It has a unique age-specific migration profile, and, despite being the pinnacle of wealth concentration, luxury consumption and celebrity success, has been shown to be a massive net loser by internal migration, except, most importantly, for young adults. This also calls for explanation.
3. The patterns of gains and losses, and of the individual flows were found to be remarkably similar between the 2000–01 and 2009–10 dates. Where differences occurred, they fitted well with the notion that migration at the earlier date was reflecting buoyant employment and housing markets, whereas at the later date these employment and housing market forces were so powerfully subdued by recession as to project other patterns, notably those associated with student

migrations, into prominence. Both the underlying stability and the changes over the economic cycle also call out for explanation. It is to these explanations for internal migration, or 'drivers' of migration, in the UK that we now turn in Chapter 4.

3.15   EPILOGUE

Since writing this opening empirical section of the book I have had a chance to read Adam Dennett's PhD thesis entitled 'Understanding internal migration in Britain at the start of the 21st century' (Dennett, 2010, 2011). It is a truly impressive study; it offers us masses of detailed results, many of which are the product of lengthy and complicated calculations, and all of the material is competently and imaginatively presented. But, as will be set out below, it is my opinion that its strengths lie more in the *descriptions* of the patterns of internal migration in the UK than in the *explanations* for them.

There are very many instances in which Dennett's empirical statements coincide with my own; examples are as follows:

- the general trend towards a counter-urban flow of migrants from the largest cities towards the surrounding small towns and rural areas;
- a tendency for young adults to move up the urban hierarchy while the remainder move down the urban hierarchy; and
- the importance of student migrations.

Unfortunately, in reporting the work of others, Dennett makes some points that we now know to be flawed (for example on p. 63, about the net balances of migrants by occupation based upon non-longitudinal data that have been shown to be incorrect when longitudinal data has been used).

The main instances in which his results represent an addition to mine are as follows. First, he studies the net migration balances for areas grouped on the basis of their main socioeconomic and locational-environmental characteristics (see also Vickers, 2010). This has the marked disadvantage that one loses spatial specificity, but on the other hand, it allows a number of rather speculative interpretations in my analysis to be confirmed. A good example of this is the suggestion I made that the former coastal retirement areas (especially those in the South East) were now net migration gain areas, not just, or even primarily, because of the inflow of new retirement or near-retirement migrants, but because the deaths of the earlier elderly in-migrants were creating affordable housing opportunities for young families to move in. Of all his area types, 'coastal Britain' had the highest net migration gain in 2000–01 (+6.7 per 1000), higher even than 'rural Britain' (at +3.6) or 'young and vibrant cities' (+3.4), and the net migration rates for those aged 0–15 and 30–44 in 'coastal Britain' were +9.8 and +10.3 per 1000 respectively. Another example is the 'commuter belt' category. One would expect net migration losses of those aged 16–29 from 'rural Britain' (–29.4) and from 'industrial legacy' areas (–15.9), but the rate of loss from the 'commuter belt' was also remarkably high at –16.7 per 1000. This conforms well with the emphasis in my analysis of these areas as the major source regions for university student migrants, many of whom will not return to their home towns and villages, but will move on to London and to other large cities.

Second, despite arguing (p. 72) that 'since the (area) classification (referred to above) does not incorporate any migration variables it provides a framework for migration analysis which is independent of the influence of a migration dimension', Dennett then proceeds to develop an area classification that *is* based on migration variables. He identifies eight clusters of local authority districts or 'migration regions' (I have placed in parentheses the counties that I focused upon above that nicely demonstrate the migration features of these types of areas): (1) areas characterized by coastal and rural retirement migrants (Cornwall); (2) low-mobility Britain (Merseyside); (3) student towns and cities (Durham, Tyne and Wear, Sheffield); (4) areas of moderate mobility (these tend to be towns/ areas without universities) (Shropshire, Wiltshire); (5) declining industrial, working-class, local Britain (Tees); (6) footloose, middle-class, commuter Britain (Buckinghamshire, Berkshire); (7) dynamic London (London (Camden and Islington)); and (8) areas characterized by successful family in-migrants (Northumberland; Norfolk). I think it would be fair to say that this section of the thesis confirms the selection of counties that I made; it does not contain categories that would require me to alter or extend that selection.

Finally, having used the 2001 Special Migration Statistics for the first two parts of the thesis, Dennett turns to the NHSCR for the period 1998–99 to 2007–08 to study migration distances, and to move towards an explanation of UK internal migration flows. On migration distances, his results once again confirm those reported above, notably in relation to the flows into and out of industrial towns and cities (short distance), the flows into and out of university cities (long distance at least for people aged 15–29) and the flows into and out of London (long in, short out). When, however, he attempts to connect the migration flows of the 1998–99 to 2007–08 period to unemployment rates and housing costs, he comes to conclusions that simply do not match the facts. In particular, his interpretations of these relationships would mean that, as unemployment rose and house prices fell in the years following 2007–08, migration rates *should* have gone up. They in fact came down, and sharply so.

This point brings me to my final comment on this major work. The strength of the detailed empirical analyses is not in question, but it is not, in my opinion, matched by the quality of the interpretation of the results. Dennett is, despite the warning that he gave himself that 'age in itself is really a proxy for the real influences acting on migrants related to their stage in the life course' (p. 236), almost obsessed with age-specific internal migration rates, and with their related life course transitions. It is significant in this respect that the sub-title of his final substantive chapter is 'From spatial interaction to life course explanations', but life course transitions represent only one of the 'drivers' of migration, and arguably quite a minor one at that. Where in this study are the really important drivers of migration? Where is the changing political economy of the society within which these internal migration flows are embedded? Social class makes an appearance in the definition of the migration regions, but where is social class as a massive influence (through expectations, social capital and resources) on the decision to migrate and on the choice of migration destination? Where are local and provincial cultural differences – the UK is an intensely patterned palimpsest of lifestyles, values and beliefs? And, above all, where are the UK's complex, shifting urban and regional economies? We should be very grateful for the masses of data that Dennett has unearthed and processed for us, but the immense task of explaining what has been revealed remains, unfortunately, largely undone!

PART II

UK internal migration: processes and trends

The purpose of Part II is, in a sense, to go 'back to basics'. It is a search for good reasons why the UK internal migration flows should take the forms that they do. It draws upon a wide literature, tries to sift the useful ideas from the less useful ones and adds a number of ideas that come out of my own research. So it is a literature review, but it is also much more that; it is, essentially, a set of judgements about what is really important in explaining the patterns described in Part I.

4. Economic drivers of internal migration

4.1 INTRODUCTION

When it comes to migration there is nothing more basic than the political economy of a country. The UK is primarily a capitalist society. Large private sector companies produce goods and services, or speculate and rent-seek, to make a profit. The investment decisions taken by these companies fix, directly or indirectly, the locations of employment and of related wealth-making opportunities across many sectors of the economy, including, indirectly, the public sector. Jobs in turn affect where people choose to live, or, to varying degrees, are forced to live. Migration from one area to another within the UK is, therefore, very largely determined by these location decisions, and by the need for people to obtain employment in the first place, or to improve their, and their families', living standards. They do this by migrating from a place where job prospects (such as pay, promotion possibilities, security of employment, working conditions, etc.) are poor, to one where they are good (Donovan et al., 2002). This means that migrants typically move from those places that are stagnating through a lack of investment, or are being run down by disinvestment, to those places that are being boosted by new investment. At the same time, recognizing the importance of labour costs to their overall profitability, and facing the reluctance of workers to leave their home communities, companies will often seek out for investment purposes those places that have reserves of cheap and easily managed labour (Green, 2004). In this way, workers move to the work *and* work moves to the workers. Finally, we can assert by way of introduction, that the economic drivers of internal migration produce different outcomes depending on whether they operate largely through the labour market or largely through the housing market: those that work through the labour market tend to produce longer-distance moves (between city-regions), whereas those that work through the housing market tend to produce shorter-distance moves (within city-regions) (Gordon, 1982).

Most writers about internal migration in a country like the UK would probably not place such a strong emphasis on the capitalist nature of the political economy as I do, but it is commonly agreed that the economic drivers of migration flows are paramount. Take, for example, the best textbook on migration – that written by Paul Boyle, Keith Halfacree and Vaughan Robinson (Boyle et al., 1998). The importance of economic drivers of migration is expressed by the fact that the first substantive chapter in their book is devoted to 'migration and employment'. In it, they discuss the neoclassical economic approach to the analysis of migration flows with its emphasis on migration as an adjustment to labour market inequalities in wages and unemployment. Then they outline the main economic models of internal migration in developed countries, including the modified gravity model (Lowry model) discussed in Chapter 1 above.

The economic analysis and modelling of internal migration in the UK has a long history (Ravenstein, 1885; Lind, 1969), but perhaps the most notable effort was that made more recently by a large team of geographers and economists mostly drawn from the universities of Newcastle and Leeds (Champion et al., 1998). Their two-stage quantitative model (stage 1: modelling out-migration; stage 2: modelling the destinations of out-migrants) was not very different in approach from that of the modified gravity model, but instead of just two or three economic, social and environmental variables, the team included over 200! It is, therefore, not surprising, perhaps, that they conclude that migration within England and Wales 'is a highly important, yet frustratingly complex, phenomenon' (ibid., p. 25). As I hope to show below, this is something of an overstatement. Using sensible conceptual frameworks, and staying close to the data (instead of throwing everything into a statistical model that only serves to distance the observer from the reality being observed), it can be seen that internal migration processes (though often failing to conform to existing conventional theories) are both fairly straightforward and easily understood.

However, to return to Boyle et al., they then conclude their chapter on migration and employment by highlighting the benefits of taking a segmented labour market approach to migration analysis. Much of what follows in this chapter builds on this line of argument; it is based upon the important truth that there is not one integrated labour market in the UK, but many semi-independent labour sub-markets hierarchically structured by location and by class, gender, ethnicity and age (Champion and Fielding, 1992) (for useful general references on, or related to, migration theory and internal migration in the UK see Ravenstein, 1885; Lee, 1969; Lind, 1969; Masser, 1970; UK: MHLG, 1970; Fielding, 1975; OPCS, 1983; Stillwell, 1983, 1990; Molho and Gordon, 1987; Champion, 1989b, 1997, 2002, 2003; 2004a, 2005; Jones and Armitage, 1990; Coleman and Salt, 1992; Jenkins, 1992; Owen and Green, 1992; Stillwell et al., 1992,

1996; Rees and Phillips, 1996; Simpson and Middleton, 1999; Geyer, 2002; Stillwell and Duke-Williams, 2003; UK: ONS, 2005; Rees et al., 2006; Champion et al., 2007; Matheson, 2009; Dennett and Rees, 2010; Wright, 2010).

The economic drivers of migration, however, take different forms depending on the time-scale over which the economic processes operate. This is an extremely important point, but awareness of it seems surprisingly absent in the literature. The recent/current economic crisis has been largely interpreted as being the result of a particularly severe downturn in the short-term business cycle consequent upon the sudden loss of confidence in the value of financial assets. It is not surprising, then, that the ideas about the impacts, actual and expected, on migration, have been drawn from our knowledge of how migration varies across the course of the business cycle.

But what if we are witnessing, at the same time, the effects of two other sets of economic processes – processes that operate over time-scales that are very different from the business cycle? I refer here to economic restructuring, that is, the medium-term restructuring of production accompanied by changes in the spatial division of labour, which is typically periodized into phases that last between two and four times the length of a business cycle; and deep structural processes, which are reflected in long-term shifts in the underlying geographies of wealth and power, which are typically played out over the period of a person's lifespan.

This complicates matters. It means that any single migration flow might be visualized as being composed of three sub-flows where each sub-flow is driven by a different set of economic processes. It is also likely that the composition of flows will vary one from another, even perhaps within a single dyadic pair of regions/nations (i.e., the flow from i to j will have a different composition of time-specific processes than the flow from j to i). I can illustrate these arguments by referring to the case of inter-regional migration flows between the London city-region (the old official 'South East Region') and the rest of England and Wales during the period 1970–90 (see Fielding, 1993, p. 140). The flows *from* the South East varied greatly through the business cycle, with high flows during boom years and low flows during recession. The flows *to* the South East varied much less; they went up a little during boom years but dipped only slightly during recession. This resulted in something of a paradox: even when it was the high performance of the London economy that produced the high national economic growth, during boom years the South East was a significant net loser by migration; conversely, during recession it was a slight net gainer by migration (please note how much this situation is at odds with the schema set out below).

The paradox is resolved when we take into account who it was that was moving and what processes were driving their migration. Those moving to the South East tended to be young, well-educated adults starting out on their middle-class careers. Their migration to the South East was seemingly almost unaffected by the ups and downs of the region's labour and property markets. They can be seen as participants in the long-term 'deep structural' escalator region process, shaping their middle-class careers by attaching themselves to the favourable social promotion prospects offered by the South East region's labour market. Those leaving the region also tended to be biased towards the middle class, but were on average much older. As the owners of housing property assets, they would be expected to choose a time of departure that maximized their financial gain. During recession, they either could not sell their houses at all, or were forced to accept low prices, so their mobility was low, but during the boom, they could 'surf the high house price wave' as it started out from the South East region and eventually spread to the rest of the country (Owen, 1992; Thomas, 1993; Meen, 1999). They could sell high and buy low, thus realizing their financial assets from migration to the greatest degree possible. Clearly, their migration was being driven, to a significant extent, by the business cycle process. Please note that it is entirely feasible for processes at different levels to counteract one another; this complexity cannot, nor should not, be avoided.

Figure 4.1 provides the conceptual framework for this line of argument (much of what follows in the opening section of this chapter is taken from Fielding, 2010). It summarizes the economic processes at each of the three levels (conjunctural, restructuring and deep structural) over the period 1950–2010, while also setting out their migration effects in high-income regions/countries.

4.2   THE ROLE OF THE BUSINESS CYCLE

At the first or top level are economic processes that involve fairly sudden changes, typically those associated with the business cycle:

Stage 1
Within a matter of months business confidence can shift from pessimism to optimism; investment suddenly increases, workers are recruited, unemployment falls, house prices start to rise, the building sector is busy and consumer confidence returns. In a region or country where this is happening, it is likely that in-migration or immigration will start rising from a low level as migrants begin to arrive to take advantage of the good

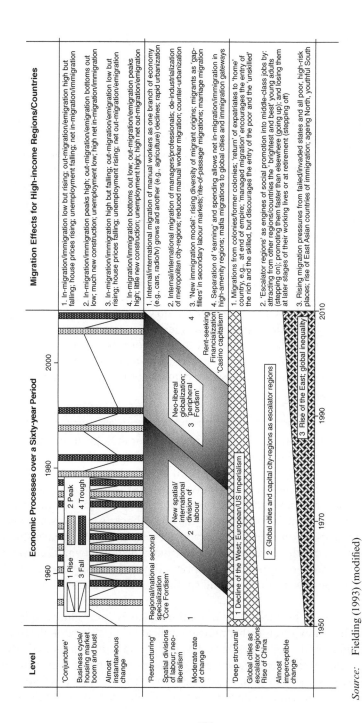

Source: Fielding (1993) (modified)

Figure 4.1 The simple conceptual framework

employment opportunities. At the same time, those who would otherwise have left, decide to stay. So net in-migration or immigration would be the expected result.

Stage 2

At the peak of the business cycle, in-migration or immigration is at a high level, and out-migration or emigration is at a low level. So high net migration gain occurs. This is typically accompanied by labour shortages, wage rate increases, high labour mobility between firms and sectors and low unemployment – in short, a fluid, dynamic labour market. This is matched, in turn, by a fluid, dynamic housing and property market as individual home owners trade up, new houses are built and new entrants to the housing market abound. Both social and spatial mobility are high.

Stage 3

It does not last. Profits begin to fall, workers are laid off, business and consumer confidence disappears, houses do not sell and unemployment begins to rise. Suddenly the region or country is no longer so attractive as a migration destination, and, perhaps fearing worse to come, some of its residents consider the possibility of looking for a better life elsewhere. As in-migration or immigration stalls and out-migration or emigration rises, the region or country shifts from being a net gainer by migration to become a net loser.

Stage 4

At the trough of the business cycle, in-migration or immigration is at a low level, and out-migration or emigration is at a high level. So net migration loss occurs. Typically, this is accompanied by very low turnovers in both the labour and housing markets. Individuals tend to retrench – hold on to the job that they have got; hold on to the house they live in – and wait for better times. Firms also retrench – they hold back from investing, and close down loss-making parts of their businesses. Unemployment is high and consumer confidence reaches rock bottom. The housing market seizes up as new entrants disappear, house prices dip and existing owners find few potential buyers. Both social and spatial mobility are low.

This picture of the business cycle/migration nexus is simple and straightforward. The real world is rather more complicated. First, as globalization has proceeded and economies have become increasingly connected, the business cycles of different regions and countries have become ever more synchronized. So, it is no longer generally the case that as one region or country enters a downturn (stage 3), others will offer new opportunities as they enter an upturn (stage 1). They tend now to go up and down together. This means that a laid-off worker in one place is less likely than before to out-migrate or emigrate, because lay-offs are now also occurring in the places to which he or she might potentially migrate.

Second, until now, this analysis has ignored the differences between internal migration and international migration. But national borders matter enormously. Internal migrants can migrate to their home region when times are bad, confident in the knowledge that, when times improve, they can return again to the high-income region. International migrants (or more accurately, migrants across the boundaries of free movement areas), on the other hand, may well decide not to leave the high-income country they live in now, for fear that they will not be allowed to re-enter in the future.

4.3 THE ROLE OF ECONOMIC RESTRUCTURING

At the second or middle level of Figure 4.1 are economic processes that involve slower changes, typically those associated with restructuring:

Period 1 (lasting from the end of World War II until about 1970)
In the early post-war period, national economies were very largely bounded by national territories. In Western Europe and North America (later joined by Japan), a Fordist mode of production/regime of accumulation dominated. The term 'Fordist' is used because the economies were characterized by leading sectors that mass-produced standardized products for mass markets (for example, cars, 'white' goods, radio/television). These leading sectors were very predominantly located in the largest city-regions of the most economically advanced countries. Their rapid growth attracted manual workers from the regions where industries were in decline, or at least were shedding labour. Thus, mass migrations occurred from rural agricultural and 'old industrial' regions towards the expanding high-growth metropolitan city-regions (Champion, 1975). There was an international dimension to this process as well. Migrants left the largely agricultural countries of peripheral Europe (Ireland, Spain, Portugal, Italy, Greece, Yugoslavia and Turkey) for the largely industrial countries of North West Europe (West Germany, France, United Kingdom and Benelux). The spatial division of labour during this period is described as 'regional sectoral specialization'. This is because each region specialized in producing those goods and services for which it had particular natural resources, locational advantages, technical skills, or product-specific cultural capital. Theoretically speaking, this spatial division of labour

equated with the social division of labour; that is, the division of labour that is brought about through market exchange.

Period 2 (from about 1955 to 1990)

Superimposed upon this production system, partially replacing it, but also coexisting with it, emerged a 'new spatial division of labour'. As companies and other organizations grew into multi-location, multi-product and increasingly multinational corporations or organizations, they began to separate out their activities to take advantage of the areal differentiation (geography) of the territories over which they operated. Their head offices gravitated to the largest metropolitan cities (and especially to the emerging global cities of London, New York and Tokyo). Their research and development activities were located in nearby/easily accessible high-amenity regions – environments that would attract highly paid technical and scientific personnel; and their routine production or activities were developed in those places, typically peripheral regions, rural areas and old industrial regions, where large reserves of cheap, 'raw' labour existed. In the UK, the geography of this process was complex in detail, but simple in its broad features; head offices and their associated producer services (such as financial, legal and marketing services) clustered in London; research and development and high-technology activities clustered along the M4 and M11 motorway corridors; and routine assembly production and back office activities took place in the peripheral regions, including old industrial regions such as South Wales and North East England. Since this process often brought work to the workers through the spatial decentralization of productive investment, manual worker migrations tended to decline, while the migration of 'functionaries' – the professional, managerial and technical staff required to coordinate and operationalize this complex, spatially extended system – tended to increase. And as this new spatial division of labour spilled over international borders, and began to involve far-flung countries as locations of routine production (attracted by very low labour costs and the low levels/absence of taxation and regulation), it became the 'new international division of labour'. A major driver of this restructuring of production was the high costs of production in advanced industrial countries, and above all, in the metropolitan regions of those countries. This led to a de-industrialization of, and disinvestment from, those cities, and then to a 'hollowing out' of the economies of those countries, resulting in a *counter-urbanization* net migration trend within national territories (Fielding, 1982, 1989), and to the end of guest-worker migrations of manual workers to the leading sectors of the core economies internationally. This spatial division of labour equated with the technical division of labour, that is, the planned division of labour within the organization.

Period 3 (1975 to 2010)

How can one characterize the more recent period of economic restructuring? At the sub-national level, the dominant feature of the earlier periods was that, in very different ways, the production activities were intimately linked to one another either (1) through market exchange (regional sectoral specialization) or (2) through the planned separation of tasks (new spatial division of labour). After the mid-1970s, however, the relationships between regional economies within a national territory could probably best be described as 'regional functional disconnection'. At the local level this resulted in the (seemingly) chance co-location of functionally unrelated economic activities. At the regional level it produced, what were to many commentators, disconcerting degrees of disconnection as, for example, in the case of the London/South East economy, where its dominant role as a global financial centre marked it out as almost a 'different country' from the rest of the UK (Massey, 2007, especially Chapter 5; Jones and Green, 2009; Erturk et al., 2011; see also Champion and Townsend, 2011). The key to all this was, of course, a new level of globalization – a neo-liberal globalization.

Period 4 (since about 1995)

It is more difficult to characterize the present than the past, but there are, surely, a number of things that can be said about the economic restructuring trends of the last 15 years. First, it is clear that, until the crisis came to a head in 2008, neo-liberal globalization proceeded apace. It is also clear, however, that the basis of profitability came to be located much less in material production and much more in the production of immaterial goods (see Communion et al., 2010 on the 'creative industries'). Some have gone so far as to characterize the recent period as one of 'cognitive capitalism' – that is, as a third stage of capitalism, following on from mercantile capitalism and industrial capitalism (Vercelloni, 2010). I do not support this approach in its entirety, but I take two of its constituent arguments very seriously: the first is that we have recently witnessed an extraordinary extension of the commoditization and financialization of social relations (for example, caring for people, knowledge exchange), so that much of what was previously free and was provided by individuals and collectivities in a spirit of mutuality as part of what it meant to live in a civilized society, is now subject to private (often corporate) ownership, the forces of the market and the profit motive. The second is the renewed importance of rent and rent-seeking behaviour. The geography of successful financialization (e.g., the development of risky innovative financial products – hence 'casino capitalism') and of rent-seeking systems of profit-making is highly specific; it is concentrated in a relatively small number of global/world cities such as New York and London. And the potential gains to individuals who succeed in these activities are astounding. It is not surprising, therefore, that these cities have become migration magnets for the bright, the ambitious, the cunning and the unscrupulous. With such concentrations of easily won wealth, cities such as these, along with 'gateway' cities (major 'ports of entry' into the high-income countries), have also become attractive locations for those who 'work' in organized crime syndicates.

The migration effects of these latest two stages of capitalist development are not, however, confined to the big financial centres. The spatial separation of the 'earning' of unearned income from the spending of it, boosted by the rising share of unearned income as a share of total income (Glynn, 2007; International Labour Office, 2010), allows the development of high-amenity areas and their significant net in-migration/immigration rates; often despite the (relative) absence of locally based economic activity. This extremely significant, but surprisingly unrecognized, change partially explains the net migration gains of the UK's high-amenity regions such as South West England (and also, of course, the attractiveness of London to international migrants).

4.4   THE ROLE OF DEEP STRUCTURAL FORCES

At the third or bottom level of Figure 4.1 are economic processes that involve changes that are so slow that they are almost imperceptible, typically those associated with the underlying geography of wealth and power:

In the early post-World War II period, patterns of international migrations were still greatly channelled by colonial and quasi-colonial links between the wealthy countries of Europe and North America and their respective 'spheres of influence' in Africa/South Asia and Latin America. Over time these connections have weakened. There are now communities of Congolese in London, Sri Lankans in Copenhagen and Filipinos in Rome. But more important than this, the massive incentive to migrate from the risky, low-income countries to the safe, high-income ones, is increasingly matched by immigration controls in the latter that allow the rich and highly skilled migrants in, but keep the poor and 'unskilled' migrants out. Such efforts to create 'fortresses' of wealth and privilege have only been partially successful – there are just too many secondary and black economy, dirty, boring and generally unpleasant jobs to be done, not just in the major cities but also in certain rural areas (Green et al., 2009)! Why is this important for internal migration? It is now widely recognized that the distribution of immigrant settlement acts as a driver of internal migration (and vice versa of course) (Salt and Kitching, 1992;

Hatton and Tani, 2005). There is a fairly close *inverse* statistical relationship at the urban and regional level between the proportion of the population that are foreign born on the one hand, and the net internal migration rate on the other (places that have few foreign born tend to have high net internal migration gains, places that have many foreign born tend to have high net internal migration losses) (King et al., 2010, pp. 56–7).

Throughout the 60-year period since 1950, however, there has been one migration constant – the strong determination of the 'brightest and the best' to attach themselves to those places that can ensure their upward social mobility (irrespective of the size of their foreign-born population). There is a kind of circulatory system that links social and geographical mobility during an individual's life course, encapsulated in the concept of the 'escalator region' (Fielding, 1992b, 2007). Escalator regions are regions/countries that usually contain large metropolitan cities (for example, global cities such as London, New York and Tokyo), and that act as 'engines' of promotion into middle- and upper-class jobs. They do this by (1) attracting from other regions/countries through in-migration a large number of educated and ambitious young adults at the start of their working lives (akin to stepping on the escalator); (2) promoting these young people at rates that are higher than those found in other regions of the country/other countries (akin to being taken up by the escalator); (3) losing through out-migration (sometimes back to the region/country of origin) a significant proportion of these upwardly mobile people at later stages of their working lives or at, or close to, retirement (akin to stepping off the escalator) (Dunford and Fielding, 1997; but see also Hoare, 1994; Hoggart, 1997; Findlay et al., 2002, 2008; Phillips, 2002, 2005, 2007).

Finally, in a grotesquely unequal world, one of the near constants of migration is the pressure to escape poverty, poor health and insecurity. In the UK, despite the regional inequalities being a whole order of magnitude less, this has resulted in southward migration across the North/South divide, added to by the strong incentive over the 30 years or so after 1969, to escape the 'troubles' in Northern Ireland (but see Compton, 1992). These near constancies tend to suppress the impacts of both the business cycle and economic restructuring (but so do other factors – see Fielding, 1997); the push factors that operated to cause internal migration from the North and West towards the South and East in search of work and better living standards remained strong throughout the period (Johnston, 1989; Coombes and Charlton, 1992; Coe and Jones, 2010). A splendid representation of these spatial inequalities in wealth is provided by the map of inheritance-tax-paying estates per 1000 persons dying in Dorling and Thomas's *Bankrupt Britain* (Dorling and Thomas, 2011).

As with all conceptual frameworks, the strengths of this system also result in some weaknesses. By separating out in a rather rigid way the differences between the economic processes operating over different time periods, the impression might have been given that no interaction between them is possible. But, whilst migration trends are largely driven by medium- and long-term determinants, crises can sometimes have long-term effects if they trigger changes in government policies or structural economic change, or if short-run migrations become long term due to social network effects (Green and Winters, 2010).

4.5   MIGRATION AND UNEMPLOYMENT

Having set out a broad framework for examining the economic drivers of internal migration in the UK, the next step is to turn to three cross-cutting forces or processes that, although very important, do not operate entirely in the way that economic logic might suggest.

The first is the impact of unemployment on migration. Economic logic would dictate that the unemployed would be the most mobile of all social groups (Salt, 1984; Pissarides and Wadsworth, 1989; Jackman and Savouri, 1992). It is true that the unemployed tend to be rather more geographically mobile than the social groups from which they are largely drawn. But since these groups (those in blue-collar working-class jobs and those living in social housing) are, on average, very spatially immobile, the effect of their higher mobility is only to bring them up to about, or slightly above, the average inter-regional migration rate for the population as a whole (Fielding, 2007). Unemployed men and women (only about one in ten of whom own bicycles) usually have too little information on opportunities elsewhere, too little money to effect a successful migration, too few contacts in potential migration destinations, and above all are too dependent on the support of their local families and communities, to risk out-migration (Kitching, 1990). The effect of this is somewhat paradoxical: regions or cities with high unemployment rates tend to experience net migration losses, but the people who are leaving are predominantly those who are already in secure, well-paid employment, or are in those social groups that will have little difficulty in finding secure, well-paid employment.

4.6   THE ROLE OF THE HOUSING MARKET

The second is the impact of housing market structure and land and property processes on migration. Some of these have already been mentioned above. Economic logic would dictate that those who own their homes would be far less geographically mobile than those who rent. After all, the owners have typically made a massive financial and psychological commitment to a particular property through its purchase, and moreover it is widely recognized that the transaction costs of moving within owner occupation are very high indeed. Furthermore, a significant proportion of renters are using the private rental sector only for as long as it takes them to effect a transition into home ownership or to move from one already owned house to another.

Yet the data tell a different story (Forrest, 1987; Forrest et al., 1991; Salt, 1991; Hamnett, 1992; Munro, 1992; Boyle, 1995; Tilling, 1995; Bate et al., 2000). Until fairly recently, the tax advantages of owner occupation, the enormous wealth accumulation potential of trading up in the housing market (and then achieving large equity release through re-mortgaging the property, or through trading down at a later stage) and the writing off of the cost of borrowing through inflation, meant that, if you were financially capable of being a home owner, you would, during most of this period, be extremely ill-advised not to be one (Saunders, 1990). And since the economic benefits of owner occupation were closely associated with the purchase, upgrading and selling of housing property, high mobility was built into the process. It is perhaps not so surprising then that the inter-regional migration rates for home owners are very much higher than those for the renters of social housing, and also higher than those for long-term renters in the private sector (Fielding, 1992a; on the housing problems of non-home owner job seekers see Conway and Ramsey, 1986). This is so despite the very real barrier to inter-regional migration that high housing costs in South East England represent (Muellbauer and Murphy, 1988; Gordon, 1990; Boyle, 1998), with those high prices boosted by international migration (Nygaard, 2011). The UK housing system is a significant driver of internal migration, and, as was alluded to earlier, not just for short distance (i.e., intra-regional) moves.

4.7 STUDENT MIGRATION

Over the last 50 years the UK has experienced a doubling, and then a doubling again, of the proportion of 18-year-olds who go on to university. This has greatly affected patterns of internal migration, has transformed the economies and cultures of many towns and cities (such as resort and retirement cities like Brighton), and has resulted in the 'studentification' of parts of the inner areas of almost all of the UK's largest cities (Hoare, 1991; Lundholm, 2007; Smith and Holt, 2007; Duke-Williams, 2009; Faggian and McCann, 2009a, 2009b; Munro et al., 2009; Hoare and Corver, 2010).

But higher education as an economic driver of migration is not quite as might be expected. In most countries that have a very dominant capital city-region (such as France, Austria, Japan and South Korea), there is a massive net migration gain of students by the capital city-region. But in the UK things are very different: each of the three regions of south-eastern England (East of England, London, and the South East) is a major net loser by student migration; that is, more 18-year-olds leave these regions to study elsewhere in England than 18-year-olds from elsewhere in England leave to study in these regions (HEFCE, 2010). It is true, in line with the escalator region metaphor discussed above, that, on graduating from university in one of these other regions, very many students migrate to the greater South East as they take up employment in the London labour market (Abreu et al., 2009; Mosca and Wright, 2010). But many do not; they put down roots during their three or four years at university (often including partial entry into the local labour market), and then seek employment in the city in which they have studied, or nearby (Faggian and McCann, 2006).

To summarize, through the great increase in student numbers, their very distinctive regional distribution, and their tendency to insert themselves into their local labour markets during their studies and at graduation, higher education has become an important economic driver of internal migration in the UK.

4.8   CONCLUSION

Despite the arguments (1) that the existence of social welfare provision dulls the incentive to migrate for work purposes – because it is possible to survive unemployment or low wages in situ; and (2) that people in affluent societies come to prioritize lifestyle ambitions over those related to money and career, the economic drivers of internal migration in the UK are of absolutely central importance. This is so despite the fact that, as has been demonstrated, these drivers do not always operate entirely in the manner expected on the basis of economic logic.

5. Social, demographic and political drivers of migration

5.1 INTRODUCTION

The UK is a highly socially stratified society: it is fundamentally divided by social class and is further differentiated according to gender and sexuality, culture and ethnicity, and age and ability. These divisions and differences act, sometimes in complex ways, as drivers of internal migration in the UK.

5.2 SOCIAL CLASS: SOCIAL MOBILITY AND GEOGRAPHICAL MOBILITY

In an area of the social sciences in which paradoxes abound (some have already been discussed above), perhaps the strangest paradox of all is that, in general, those who need to migrate the most (that is, the poor and the powerless) tend to migrate the least, while those who need to migrate the least (because they are in well-paid, secure employment and own their own houses), tend to migrate the most.

Much of the rest of this sub-section is based on Fielding (1992a), and Fielding (1995) from which Table 5.1 is taken.

The small group composed of those who are very wealthy and powerful (not identified separately in Table 5.1) tend to own properties in several regions and countries; they would tend to move regularly between, for example, a house or apartment in London, a country house or estate in the Cotswolds or the West Country, and a luxury holiday home in Southern Europe or the Caribbean. We could perhaps say that they lead 'peripatetic' lives rather than 'migratory' ones.

If we conceptualize the large middle class as having three sub-divisions: (1) managers, (2) professionals and (3) the petty bourgeoisie (the self-employed and owners of small and medium-sized businesses), then two of these groups, the managers and professionals, are generally highly mobile, both socially and geographically. They are what sociologists call 'spiralists', that is, they achieve upward social mobility by migrating from

Migration in Britain

Table 5.1   *Inter-regional migration rates by social class (England and Wales = 100)*

	Population %	In Labour Market in 1991	In Labour Market in 1981 & 1991	In Labour Market in Same Class in 1981 & 1991
Professionals	15.2	185	162	204
Managers	11.3	151	159	195
Petty bourgeoisie	9.7	85	94	59
White-collar working class	24.5	89	89	96
Blue-collar working class	29.5	52	50	46
Unemployed	9.9	95	112	121
Total	100.0	100	100	100

Source: OPCS Longitudinal Study (1991) (Crown Copyright Reserved).

one city or region to another as they pursue career advancement (Bell, 1968). This career advancement often takes place within the organiza-tion, and indeed, intra-organizational transfers account for a large share of inter-regional migration in the UK (Johnson and Salt, 1980a; Salt, 1990; Flowerdew, 1992). The migration of managers and professionals is made easier by (1) the fact that increasingly over time these people had already migrated away from their home regions as university students; and (2) the fact that, for much of the recent period, one could achieve increases in household wealth through trading up in the housing market (see above). But, for professionals much more than for managers, there is also a serious drawback with high inter-regional mobility: how does one match the career expectations of both parties in a dual-career household when migration is very likely to be to the career advantage of one of them, but to the disadvantage of the other (Snaith, 1990; Green, 1992a, 1995, 1997)?

In sharp contrast to the managers and professionals, those who are self-employed or own small or medium-sized businesses tend to be very geographically immobile. This is because their success often depends on building up trust, a positive personal reputation, strong local social net-works, good working relations with nearby suppliers and customers and a well-developed knowledge of the local area. There is, however, significant inter-regional migration of people as they switch into the petty bourgeoi-sie, for example, as they set up a small business in a high-amenity region (see Bosworth, 2010 on in-migrant counter-urbanizing entrepreneurs in rural North East England). Many such people were formerly managers or professionals in London, or in a major metropolitan city.

We can conceptualize the largest class of all, the working class, as also having three sub-divisions: (1) white-collar working class, (2) blue-collar working class and (3) the unemployed. Since the migration of the unemployed has already been discussed in the previous chapter, attention here will focus on the two other groups. People (predominantly women) who do low-level white-collar jobs (such as routine office work, personal care jobs and serving in shops and restaurants) are only averagely mobile inter-regionally. Sometimes when they are migrants, it is because they are the 'trailing spouse or partner' in a household where the man is the dominant earner and may be migrating for career development reasons (for example, to take up a post as a manager). Many women also take on low-level white-collar jobs, sometimes on a part-time basis, when they move away from the large city and its middle-class career-type jobs and lifestyles, to move towards a small town or rural location – a move that is often associated with the decision either to start a new family, or to raise an existing one in a different environment.

Manual workers (blue-collar working class) are, on average, quite remarkably inter-regionally immobile. Some of the reasons for this have already been discussed, but there are specifically social reasons for this low spatial mobility as well as reasons related to the labour market (for example, the typically sector- and locality-specific nature of their industrial skills and workplace reputations). These social reasons include the frequently important role that family members, such as the woman's mother, play in childcare, and, more generally, the very spatially restricted nature of family and friendship networks. It is important to emphasize, however, that while this is generally the case, there are certain kinds of jobs that can have high spatial mobility built into them. Working for a construction company that has major projects in other regions or countries is the sort of case that comes to mind.

To summarize, social class stratification is a significant driver of internal migration in the UK; the social relations attached to being a manager or professional result in an inter-regional migration rate that is approximately four times that of a blue-collar worker (Fielding, 1992a, p. 230).

5.3   MIGRATION AND GENDER/SEXUALITY

The territory of the UK might appear from the outside to be uniform with respect to gender relations and sexual identities, but this is not the case. It is highly patterned, first by the differential social mobility prospects for men and women, and second by the differential strengths of hetero-normativity. These regional and local differences act as drivers of migration.

In very general terms, and having adjusted for the overall difference in social promotion between men and women, women are more upwardly mobile than men in the most prosperous region of the UK, that is, London/ South East England, and in the least prosperous regions, that is, the large industrial conurbations of northern and western UK (the analysis in this sub-section is taken from Fielding, 1998b; but see also Duncan and Smith, 2002). They are less upwardly mobile than men in the vast rural and small town hinterlands of the country's largest cities, that is, the remainder of the UK space. This, unsurprisingly, correlates fairly closely with patriarchy and with family formation behaviour. For example, the opportunity cost of marriage followed by full-time childcare for a well-educated, ambitious woman (perhaps especially for one who possesses 'erotic capital' – Hakim, 2010) living in London is almost inconceivably high. The result of this and related arguments, expressed in a highly simplified manner, is a threefold regionalization: London is a low-patriarchy, low-familism region; the extended small town and rural hinterlands of major cities are high-patriarchy, high-familism regions; and the industrial conurbations of northern and western UK are low-patriarchy, high-familism regions. These gender and family characteristics of regions are maintained and reinforced by the migration of people seeking places that conform to their underlying values and behaviours (Duncan and Smith, 2002, pp. 490–91; Grimsrud, 2011).

This last line of argument can also be applied to sexual identity. The concentrations of male homosexuals in locations of low homophobia/ hetero-normativity such as Inner London, Brighton and Edinburgh was originally built up, and is now maintained, by the migration of those seeking like-minded sexual lifestyles (for an interestingly different case see Smith and Holt, 2005).

5.4   THE ROLE OF CULTURE/ETHNICITY

The UK taken as a whole is a multicultural society in fact, if not at every time and in every place in spirit. But the differences between regions and cities are vast. For diversity in people's values and beliefs, languages and countries of birth, physical appearances and lifestyles, London is in a class of its own. Most former industrial conurbations and large provincial cities have significant ethnic minority populations, but the rest of the UK is very predominantly 'white', English speaking and of British (or Irish) ancestry (Reid and Miller, 2010).

This intensive cultural patterning of UK space is both a product of past migration, notably through the processes of settlement of international migrants coming to the UK in the post-World War II period, and of contemporary migration, notably through the selective migration of many older, conservatively minded people of British ancestry into the outer suburban, peri-urban, small town and rural hinterlands of the UK's largest cities and conurbations (sometimes described as 'white flight' in the United States; for evidence of the inverse relationship between immigration and white internal migration in the United States see Bogue et al., 2009, p. 84) (for data on the migration of different ethnic groups in the UK, showing that minority ethnic groups' migrations were often more gender-specific, and that they frequently moved less far than white groups, see Robinson, 1992, 1993; Finney and Simpson, 2008).

Once in being, this intensive cultural patterning of UK space acts a powerful driver of internal migration. For example, young adults, the most geographically mobile of all age groups, are, on average, much less averse to cultural, ethnic and lifestyle diversity than those of their parents' generation. Thus, in addition to the forces of economic necessity working through the labour and housing markets that encourage young adults to migrate to the largest cities, and especially to London, in their search for jobs and affordable rented accommodation, there are strong preferences for these places as centres of partying, fashion, furious social networking and celebrity success (notice the high turnover and churn of London's population; see Dennett and Stillwell, 2008).

5.5 MIGRATION AND THE LIFE COURSE: FAMILY FORMATION/FISSION

At the start of this chapter it was argued that no understanding of migration drivers would be complete without an awareness of the social class dimension of migration rates. The same argument applies to age (Boden, 1989; Dennett and Stillwell, 2011). The schedule of inter-regional migration rates by age is spectacular: young children are mobile because of their parents' mobility, then migration rates drop to a low level perhaps because many parents try to avoid a disruption of their children's education in the run up to school-leaving examinations. Migration rates then rise very steeply, especially so in the recent period, due to higher rates of university entrance, and remain high into the early/mid-20s. The rates are high but declining during the 30s and fall steadily in the 40s and 50s to reach a very low level before retirement. Leaving the labour market is accompanied by a small, but discernable, rise or levelling out in migration in the early/mid-60s, and, finally, rates fall again in old age, but rise significantly for the very elderly as independent living becomes impossible or very difficult to sustain.

Key life course events have different effects on migration (and vice versa – see Grundy, 1992; Warnes, 1992a; Fielding and Ishikawa, 2003; Bramley et al., 2006). The transition to adulthood, accompanied sometimes by intense efforts to achieve personal development and the 'pursuit of happiness', often involves living in another region or another country for a period of time (Waters et al., 2011). Leaving home is, on average, later than in the past, and a growing proportion of young adults, despite the higher rates of university entrance, are still living in their parental homes in their 20s and 30s. While work and study may well encourage a move to another region, finding somewhere to live usually results in a local move. On ceasing to be single, a migration almost always takes place, with, on average, longer migrations for middle-class couples than for working-class ones. An expanding family tends to produce local moves, for example to the suburbs, as the need for housing space increases (Champion and Congdon, 1992). Relationship breakdown typically implies a new migration, sometimes from a suburban or peri-urban location back to the inner city for one or both of the partners, as housing assets are divided between them (Hayes et al., 1995). A new sequence of family formation and associated residential moves may well ensue as these individuals enter second marriages or partnerships. Once again, for most people, these transitions are occurring later than in the past; marriage is less frequent and later, starting a family likewise. When reaching the end of child rearing, a couple may well decide that they do not want to live any longer in a large house (or 'empty nest'), but prefer to realize some of their housing assets by 'trading down' in the housing market. If this process roughly coincides with leaving the labour market altogether, a long-distance migration (or even emigration) may result.

5.6 RETIREMENT MIGRATION

Retirement migration has been singled out for special attention because it is such an exceptional and important migration stream (see Grundy, 1987; Rees, 1992; Warnes, 1992b; Glaser and Grundy, 1998; Champion, 2004b; Green, 2006; Stockdale, 2006a; and Brown and Glasgow, 2008 for a useful account of rural retirement migration in the United States). It is exceptional because it is decoupled from the employment drivers of migration, and it is important because many retirement migrants are asset and income rich, and their migration has very significant impacts on the local economies of the places where they choose to settle. They create employment opportunities, sustain services and invest in housing infrastructure, for example in rural and peripheral regions where such job opportunities and infrastructure investments are often badly needed. However, the migration of the over 50s is not totally dominated by retirement migration or migration consequent upon the loss (or losing) of independence. It is very much related to relationship change, both as a result of the death of a partner, and as a result of divorce and the formation of new relationships (Evandrou et al., 2010).

5.7 THE ROLE OF PUBLIC POLICY

In the early post-World War II period the state was fairly interventionist in matters relating to internal migration. Both Labour and Conservative governments were committed to strong regional policies favouring (1) agricultural and industrial development in rural and peripheral regions and, above all, (2) the economic regeneration of the old industrial conurbations. At a more local level, the state was a major driver of internal migration through its slum clearance and new town building programmes. There was even, for a time, a direct subsidy for labour mobility through the Employment Transfer Scheme (Johnson and Salt, 1980b).

And yet, in two very important respects, the state has acted, quite unintentionally, in ways that have raised major barriers to internal migration. The first is through social housing. The rules of access to council housing tenancies in the earlier part of the period, and to the much-reduced stock of social housing today, tend to favour the non-migratory local residents over the migratory non-local residents (Hughes and McCormick, 1981, 1987; Forrest and Murie, 1992; Bramley et al., 2004). The second is through planning policy. So difficult has it been to get land released for house-building purposes that severe shortages of skilled and unskilled labour have been allowed to choke off growth in high-growth regions (Hughes and McCormick, 1990). It is still the case today that each house built in England has to last for 226 years; this is because housing completions (at about 100 000 per annum) represent such a minute proportion of total housing stock (22.6 million dwellings) (the 'persistent inadequate supply' of housing was a key finding of the Barker Report, 2004; see also UK: Government Office for Science, 2010; and Kintrea, 2005 on housing obsolescence).

5.8   CONCLUSION

By way of conclusion we can explore through Table 5.2 the manner in which social class, housing tenure, gender, region of origin and inter-regional migration intersect to product extraordinarily different social mobility outcomes (all the following figures come from Fielding, 2007; please note that analyses of longitudinal data for later periods show very similar results).

A man who comes from an owner-occupation background, and a low-level white-collar job, if he migrates to the London city-region from elsewhere in England and Wales, has a 55 per cent chance of achieving upward social mobility into the professional or managerial middle classes within ten years. A woman who comes from a social renting background, and a blue-collar job, who lives outside the London city-region and does not migrate out of her region, has only a 3 per cent chance of achieving upward promotion into the professional or managerial middle classes within ten years. This astounding 20-fold difference in social mobility out-comes reflects (1) the unequal nature of contemporary UK society; (2) the importance of gender relations, housing processes and regional context in determining life chances; and, above all, (3) the vital link between inter-regional migration and social promotion (this conforms to studies of the 'returns to migration' literature in economics: see Boheim and Taylor, 2007; Faggian et al., 2007). The chances of upward mobility are roughly doubled if the person migrates inter-regionally. It is hardly surprising, then, that the social structure of our society, and the attempts by individuals to improve their positions within it, are such powerful drivers of UK internal migration flows.

Table 5.2 Interactions between inter-regional migration, social class, housing tenure, gender and region, as they affect entry to the professional and managerial service class. England and Wales 1971–81

		Total		Inter-regional Migrants Only	
		Total	Males only	Total	Males only
In labour market in 1971					
Total					
England & Wales	Total	11.4	12.3	23.1	26.0
	Own-occ. only	14.7	16.4	26.1	30.5
South East only	Total	13.5	15.1	28.2	32.0
	Own-occ. only	17.4	20.0	33.9	39.9
White collar only					
England & Wales	Total	18.8	31.7	31.1	45.6
	Own-occ. only	21.7	35.6	32.6	48.0
South East only	Total	19.7	32.1	35.8	49.6
	Own-occ. only	22.9	36.0	40.6	55.4
Entries from education 1971–81					
England & Wales	Total	18.3	18.2	45.7	47.9
	Own-occ. only	24.0	24.2	49.0	50.5
South East only	Total	19.0	29.8	50.5	53.7
	Own-occ. only	25.3	25.8	54.2	57.5

Notes:
a. The data refer to people in England and Wales at both dates.
b. A rate of entry into the service class is calculated by dividing the number of people entering the service class 1971–81 by the number of people in the category of origin in 1971. The rates of entry are therefore transition probabilities ×100.
c. Data for South East inter-regional migrants are for flows *to* the (old) South East region.

Source: OPCS Longitudinal Study (Crown Copyright Reserved).

6. Environmental drivers of migration

6.1 INTRODUCTION

The term 'environmental', when used in the context of drivers of migration, can be either: (1) a broader notion of 'environment' that is largely social in content, or (2) a narrower notion of 'environment' that is largely physical in content. An example of the use of the first notion, which refers to the social context of people's lives, is a phrase like 'it's the place's fault!' Here, some combination of features of the place is so threatening to one's well-being, that it provokes the powerful response of out-migration. The second is confined to 'environment' in the physical sense; that is, the combination of forces, geological, biological, meteorological and so on that make up the physical and material context of our lives. This second notion can in turn be divided into environment (a) as a strong force of fact, as for example, in the case of the presence or absence of a large reservoir of oil, or (b) as a weaker force of preference and perception, like dull skies, cold winters, fine scenery, beautiful wildlife. To take the first case: the development of North Sea oil and gas deposits, in the context of massive price rises in 1973 and 1979, led to a boom in the economies of Aberdeen and other places in eastern and north-eastern Scotland in the 1975–2000 period, which, in turn, led to significant in-migration and settlement. As this example shows, even these physical forces, both strong and weak, are not just physical in content, they cannot be satisfactorily discussed in isolation from human needs and evaluations.

6.2 MIGRATION AND THE SPATIAL INEQUALITIES IN HEALTH/LONGEVITY

The UK does have a specific geography of physical environmental threat. Low-lying areas of eastern England, for example, remain vulnerable to a repeat experience of the kind of disastrous storm surge damage that they suffered in 1953. Naturally occurring radon gas emissions, and landslides due to rotational slippage, are further examples of environmental problems that have very specific geographies within the UK. Furthermore and more generally, when the spatial distributions of poor health and an early death are examined, there is a clear tendency for the colder, wetter and cloudier northern and western regions of the UK to have higher standardized mortality rates than the warmer, dryer and sunnier south and east. It is clear to this author, however, that it is not the physical environment per se that is determining the risk of illness and death, it is social conditions and, above all, poverty that does the damage. With poverty come the many things that bring poor health and shorten one's life, especially poor-quality housing, unemployment, self-damaging behaviours such as smoking and alcohol/drug abuse, poor-quality nutrition, dangerous working conditions and so on. Yes, people who are ill and live short lives tend to live in or near to physically hazardous environments (for example, cold wet winters, flood plains and places that have high concentrations of industrial pollutants such as dioxins), but, generally speaking, it is their poverty that explains *both* their location and their short lives, not the presence of dangerous elements in their environment (Laurian, 2008).

This position has recently received support from research on the correlation between the physical characteristics of areas (which include their built environments and levels of pollution) and their standardized mortality rates (Short et al., 2011). The authors conclude 'the physical environment has some power to explain health inequalities, independent of socio-economic deprivation. However, . . . this effect is relatively weak and the results emphasise the very strong relationship that exists between health outcomes and deprivation' (ibid., p. 83). They go on to assert that the effects of the physical environment are especially great for those in 'more socially deprived groups who are likely to be less mobile and thus exposed at a greater degree to their home environments' (ibid.).

6.3   THE ROLE OF 'PLACISM', FOR EXAMPLE, THE REPUTATIONS OF PLACES FOR CRIME/ VIOLENCE

Sometimes only tenuously linked to the real dangers of living in particular places, there is a distinctive geography of places that are *thought* to be dangerous. To many people who spend their whole lives in rural village England, the inner parts of the largest cities, and conurbations more generally, are seen as crime-ridden environments where violence, theft, sexual perversion and drug addiction are the norm. This categorization of places, and by extension, the people who live in them ('placism'), is a very real phenomenon, and one that affects the decisions that people make about where they should live, and hence whether or not they should migrate to another area. Powerful mixtures of class snobbery, fear of change, racism and distrust of crowds, encourage many individuals to massively exaggerate the risks of living in the vibrant, diverse, multicultural city, and massively exaggerate also the benefits of living in the 'cricket-on-the-village-green' countryside.

6.4   LIFESTYLE MIGRATION TO HIGH-AMENITY REGIONS

Surveys of migrants' reasons for migrating inter-regionally within the UK demonstrate the importance of these place preferences in their decisions. In particular, the counter-urban trend, favouring migration from the largest cities to small towns and rural areas, has been explained by many commentators as a product of the widespread attachment to the 'rural idyll' (Williams, 1985; Champion, 1987, 1989a, 1994, 1998; Hickingbotham and Strachan, 1991; Jones, 1992; Halliday and Coombes, 1995; Boyle and Halfacree, 1998; Short and Stockdale, 1999; Stockdale et al., 2000; Champion and Fisher, 2003; Mitchell, 2004; Stockdale and Findlay, 2004; Stockdale, 2006b, 2010; Hoggart, 2007; Walford, 2007; Halfacree, 2008; Kowalczuk, 2010; but see Spencer, 1997; Lewis, 2000; Stockdale, 2002a, 2002b and 2004 and Milbourne, 2007 on rural poverty and the continuing migration of young people away from these rural areas; Satsangi et al., 2010 on rural housing problems; and Smith, 2002 on 'rural gatekeepers' shaping who moves in to rural areas).

There are good reasons for accepting this emphasis on place preferences: (1) with an improvement in living standards, the argument goes, people become less interested in earning that little extra money, and more interested in establishing a convivial lifestyle, one that matches their values and priorities (Jones et al., 1986; Findlay and Rogerson, 1993; Murdoch and Day, 1998); and (2) as the population ages, so more and more people are retired or semi-retired and therefore no longer need to live in job-rich (mostly large urban or metropolitan) environments. They can 'live the dream' of retiring to a quiet, safe, high-amenity rural environment to concentrate on their outdoor hobby interests (such as gardening, golf, hill-walking, sailing, etc.) (Boyle, 1997; Millington, 2000; Benson and O'Reilly, 2009; but see Fielding, 1998a).

There are some serious problems, however, with this kind of survey-based analysis. First, we can hardly expect people to be honest about, or even sometimes aware of, their migration motives. This is especially so if such motives include, say, an avoidance of foreigners (for fear of being labelled a racist), or a wish to control family members (for fear of being labelled authoritarian). Second, such surveys often ignore the necessary conditions for such a migration. These include: (1) sufficient wealth accumulation to successfully execute the migration; (2) for those still dependent on earned income, the improvements in transport and communications that make it possible to live in a desired environment while still retaining close links with city-based employment (for example, by working from home on certain days in the week); and (3) the significant shift towards higher returns for capital over those for labour. This means that many can afford to live on unearned income, geographically very separate from where the workers who generated that income are located (such as in the major cities of the UK or in developing countries).

6.5   THE ROLE OF CLIMATE/WEATHER

Are migrants within the UK driven by the climate and weather differences between places? There is, of course, a common preference for warm and sunny locations over cold and cloudy ones, and net out-migration rates are indeed higher for wetter, colder areas (UK: Office of the Deputy Prime Minister, 2002, p. 105). But, in a very small number of cases, the climate driver can be much more specific. An example would be where someone has a breathing-related illness. It could well be in their interest to move to an environment where the air is less polluted and the houses and workplaces are warmer and drier.

6.6   CONCLUSION

To summarize, environmental drivers of internal migration in the UK are, broadly speaking, not very important when the notion of 'environmental' that is used is largely physical. The exception to this generalization is when migration is driven by natural resource developments or by major shifts in agriculture, fishing, forestry and so on. But, when the notion of 'environmental' that is used is largely social, then it can be said that much migration in the UK is driven by environmental considerations. It is essential to qualify this statement, however, by pointing out that the 'environments' to which migrants are responding, built up by media stereotyping, and drawing upon deeply rooted 'placist' traditions in British culture, may well be the grossly exaggerated ones of the imagination, rather than the actual ones on the ground.

7. The decision to migrate

7.1 INTRODUCTION

This chapter focuses on the individual migrant/non-migrant to explore the bases on which decisions to leave or to stay are made. It can reasonably be inferred from what has been written above, that personal traits such as ambition, self-confidence and courage, personal relationship success and failure, as well as personal resources (social capital) such as good knowledge of other places, and close friends and family members in other places, can greatly influence the decision to migrate.

7.2 MIGRATION AS A LEARNED BEHAVIOUR

In addition, however, migration decisions have both their own dynamism and their own rather specific contexts. A good example of the former is the strong tendency for migration to be a learned behaviour (Cairns and Smyth, 2009). By this is meant that having migrated once, it is much easier to migrate again; typically, the fear of unknown places and people is reduced, the confidence that one can cope with the psychological stresses of migration has been enhanced and experience of the practical aspects of migration, such as getting a new job and selling a house, has been gained. So linked is one migration decision to others, and so important is this in determining life chances, outlook and status that some social scientists (notably Manuel Castells; see, in particular, Castells, 1993) regard the fundamental division of contemporary society as being that between 'cosmopolitans' and 'locals', where the former have life-paths that connect them to many distant places, while the latter live out their lives in just one place.

This influence of past migration on current behaviour is seen also in rural areas. In her study of young people migrating away from, or deciding to stay in the Scottish Borders, Gill Jones finds that migrants often had a family history of migration while stayers were largely from local families; the former often could not wait to get away, while the latter are typically too attached to the area to leave even if they could do better elsewhere (Jones, 2001).

7.3   TRADE-OFFS BETWEEN MIGRATION, CIRCULATION AND COMMUTING

No clear-cut line divides migration from other kinds of spatial mobility. For a wealthy household (perhaps especially so if you are a Member of Parliament) it is sometimes quite difficult to ascertain which is one's 'primary residence'; a second home in the countryside, at the seaside, or abroad, can be a weekend or holiday retreat during a person's working life, but a home after retirement. Many lives involve quasi-migrations (such as long working holidays), or weekly or monthly shifts in location; sometimes this is work-related, as when oil workers spend periods of time offshore, armed forces personnel are posted overseas, or sales personnel spend two days a week at the company's head offices. On other occasions, multi-local living is a product of complex interpersonal relationships, such as when children live for periods of time with each of their estranged parents.

However, the site of most mobility trade-offs and compromises is between migration and commuting (Green, 1999b). As it becomes physically possible to travel over greater distances and in more directions than previously, due to faster rail transport and higher car ownership, it also becomes possible to affect a job change without changing residence, or to live in a low-housing-cost region while working in a high-housing-cost region (Cameron and Muellbauer, 1998, for example, show the significant net regional commuting gains to the South East region; see also Flowerdew and Boyle, 1992; Findlay et al., 2001; Champion et al., 2009). Add to this the increased incidence of working from an office at home, and the previous necessity to migrate on the occasion of a job change becomes much reduced. For many people long-distance commuting, with perhaps also short periods of living away from home, is being substituted for definitive migration (Green and Canny, 2003).

7.4   THE MIGRATION OF DUAL-CAREER HOUSEHOLDS

One very good reason for substituting commuting for migration is that it allows two careers to be built instead of one. Migration towards a major metropolitan region (typically of single people) tends to favour the career developments of both men and women. Migration away from a large metropolitan region generally favours male career paths but works very much to the detriment of female careers (Fielding and Halford, 1993; Lundholm, 2007). The reason for this asymmetry seems to be (at least in the past, but maybe still for managerial careers) that women, as the 'trailing spouse', are the losers by migration (Green, 1999a). The dense job opportunity landscape of a major metropolitan area such as the London region ensures that women have many career opportunities, but the sparser opportunity landscapes of non-metropolitan areas, plus the disruption of a career path consequent upon migration, damages female career development. It follows from this that dual-career households have very good reason to migrate towards, and not to migrate away from, the London region (Rabe and Taylor, 2010) (a similar argument is used to explain the low out-migration rates from the Lothian/Strathclyde region; see Belding and Hutchison, 1976; also Belfield and Morris, 1999).

If, however, the development of two careers virtually forces separation (particularly common in professional households), then a situation of 'living apart together' (LAT) can arise (Duncan and Phillips, 2010). Here, permanent co-residence is avoided by the couple maintaining two homes – homes that are located in different cities, regions or even countries, while still remaining a couple (these are sometimes called 'dual location households'; see Green et al., 1999; Hardill, 2002). With increasing academic success, higher levels of entry into the professions, and later/less childbearing, women are increasingly likely to have career paths that put geographical distance between them and their 'significant others'.

7.5   THE 'TRIPLE BIOGRAPHY' APPROACH

One of the best ways to gain an understanding of these complex relationships at the level of the individual is through the triple biography approach. By means of a lengthy interview, part of which entails the recording of all the significant events in the person's triple biography, that is, their journeys through (1) education, training and work; (2) personal relationships and family formation; and (3) the places in which they have resided, it is possible to build a picture of that individual's occupational, social and geographical mobility. Put together, clear patterns of connection emerge. Surprisingly large differences arise between cosmopolitans and locals, single people and couples, dual-career households and others. While broad economic and social forces matter enormously as the main drivers of internal migration in the UK, so also do the myriad particularities of individual migration decisions.

7.6   CONCLUSIONS TO CHAPTERS 4 TO 7

The main conclusions of these four analytical chapters (Chapters 4 to 7) of Part II of this book are that:

1.   The economic drivers of internal migration in the UK are of paramount importance. They typically imply migration for the purpose of gaining employment, or for improved terms and conditions in employment, and can be usefully grouped into (a) short-term business cycle processes; (b) medium-term restructuring processes; and (c) long-term 'deep structural' processes (such as the 'escalator region' character of the London/South East region) – and of these, the restructuring processes are particularly important (and probably the least well understood). In addition, it was shown that unemployment was far less of a driver of migration than would be expected on the basis of economic logic, and that housing was far more of a driver than expected. Student migrations were also emphasized because they had become so important in the recent period. Finally, it was pointed out that the spatial separation of the 'earning' of unearned income from the spending of it, boosted by the rising share of unearned income as a proportion of total income, helps to explain the high net in-migration gains of high-amenity areas (such as South West England), even when, as is often the case, the economic performance of these areas is poor.
2.   The social, demographic and political drivers of internal migration in the UK are also very important indeed. There are striking differences between social classes in their inter-regional migration rates. Furthermore, the link between migration and intra-generational social class mobility is particularly significant – those who move spatially tend also to succeed socially. Internal migration is also highly gendered, and there are strong links between migration, gender-specific social mobility rates and family formation behaviours. One of the key social drivers of migration is the individual's life course, with particular kinds of migration associated with each transition (for example, a suburban or peri-urban move linked to the enlargement of the family). Finally, culture and ethnicity are drivers of migration, with the same feature of a region (such as high cultural diversity) having differential effects on migration – encouraging some to move in, while encouraging others to move out.
3.   Despite the importance granted in the literature to environmental drivers of internal migration in the UK, largely based upon the results of questionnaire surveys of migrants' reasons for moving, the

judgement of this review was that environmental drivers are far less important than social drivers, which in turn are less important than economic drivers. Finally, that difficult trade-offs between migration, commuting and circulation exist for many households, but perhaps especially so for dual-career households.

8. Future migration trends in the absence of environmental change

8.1 INTRODUCTION

This chapter is highly speculative. It attempts to set out the likely trends in internal migration in the UK in the absence of environmental change. For each of the categories of migration drivers discussed in the previous chapters it asks questions like: will these drivers remain as important, become less important, or become more important in the future? Will the nature of the causal relationships that result in migration change over time? Will existing trends continue, or will new trends be likely to emerge? What are the patterns of internal migration in the UK likely to be in 20 and 50 years' time?

8.2 TRENDS IN THE ECONOMIC DRIVERS OF MIGRATION

As far as the business cycle effects on migration are concerned, it is impossible to imagine that these will disappear as long as the UK remains a predominantly capitalist society. Boom and bust most certainly have not been eradicated from the system, despite the appearance to the contrary in the late 1990s and early 2000s. So periods of high mobility coincident with economic booms, and periods of low mobility coincident with recessions are to be expected.

This brings us to the big issue – what system of production, exchange and consumption *will* dominate the UK economy over the next 20 and 50 years? To answer this question requires imagination. But this is difficult – we tend to be trapped in the present. For example, some (is this true for global climate modellers?) seem to find it easier to imagine the end of the world than the end of capitalism! But the lesson of history is that we should guard against the assumption that what seems so inevitable today will still exist tomorrow.

The likely alternatives are, in my opinion, as follows:

1. *A continuation and enhancement of global neo-liberal capitalism.* This
    seems to me to be relatively unlikely due to (a) this system's vulner-
    ability to severe crises brought about by unregulated speculation; (b)
    its ability to seriously undermine the living standards of people living
    in affluent and powerful nations (notably the United States); and (c)
    the increasing ability of economic agents to avoid the monopolistic
    and monopsonistic rent-seeking practices of Western financial and
    commercial corporations. Were it to continue, however, we would
    see also a continuation of regional functional disconnection as the
    dominant spatial division of labour. The implications of this and of
    further neo-liberal capitalism for migration within the UK are not
    easy to judge, but it would seem likely that London would continue to
    dominate the space economy, and thus continue to attract the bright-
    est and the best (and worst) from the rest of the country, but that the
    capital region would be subject to severe downturns in its economy.
    So severe might these downturns become that the metropolitan region
    might, for periods of time, experience urban crisis and hence become
    a major source of out-migration.
2. *A reversion to a purer form of production-oriented capitalism.* This
    seems to me to be much more likely, and there are powerful voices
    already supporting such a shift (often expressed as a 're-balancing of
    the economy'). The paradox is that such a shift would require very
    considerable state intervention since without such intervention the
    tendencies towards speculation, monopoly and rent-seeking would
    go unchecked. A reversion to production-oriented capitalism would
    also imply a reversion to the new spatial division of labour (the intra-
    organizational spatial separation of roles in the production system).
    The implications of this for migration are that one would expect
    moderately high levels of spatial mobility, the relative decline of the
    London city-region and a rejuvenation of the economies of industrial
    conurbations, large provincial cities and even, perhaps, the urban-
    ized countryside (as started to happen in the 1970s), thus significantly
    altering dominant migration flows.
3. *The emergence of 'third way' forms of social market capitalism.* This
    seems to me to be a moderately likely outcome. There are two forces
    that push the UK in this direction: the first is the enduring success
    in both economic and social terms of the 'Scandinavian model' of a
    mixed capitalist/state socialist system linked to liberal progressivism;
    the second is the emerging 'Beijing Consensus', at the core of which
    lies the East Asian developmental, bureaucratically authoritarian,
    highly interventionist state, linked to a closely regulated market capi-
    talism, and to a family-based social welfare system. One would expect

a combination of the new spatial division of labour and regional sectoral specialization to accompany this process. The implications of such a system for internal migration in the UK are that overall mobility would probably be less than in the two previous cases, but that enhanced urban and regional development policies would result in strong incentives to migrate to new state-sponsored investment zones associated with new and innovative forms of urban settlement.

4. *The establishment of a form of 'local socialism'.* This seems a relatively unlikely event at present, but there are four trends that are conformable with such an outcome. The first is the already existing commitment, on the part of small producers and many consumers, to both local trading and 'local production for local consumption' (partially expressed, perhaps, through the current popularity of local economic initiatives, and of informal economy activities such as car boot sales and farmers' markets). The second is the enthusiasm for the idea, partially expressed perhaps in the notion of the 'big society', that through local forms of mutual aid and cooperation many improvements in living standards and quality of life can be achieved. The third trend, closely related to this, is the developing critique that many key corporations are 'too big to fail', and that smaller, locally and collectively owned organizations would provide more *resilience* in uncertain times. Finally, the rise in the use of natural resources and new technologies as tools for power politics, and more specifically, anxieties about food security, energy security and cyber security, also propel society towards such an outcome. Higher levels of regional economic autonomy and local ownership and management of organizations would mean that both the new spatial division of labour and regional functional disconnection would disappear, or be seriously weakened. What would be left would be a milder version of regional sectoral specialization. The implications for internal migration are difficult to discern, not least because the UK is one of the most globalized countries in the world. But a general rustication of the population would be expected, along with lower levels of mobility, a decline in port cities and a major restructuring of the economies and spatial structures of London and the largest conurbations, which would probably lead to the reassertion of strong counter-urban migration flows. (Please note that a fifth alternative scenario is added below.)

After writing the passages above, I read John Urry's very interesting book entitled *Climate Change and Society* (Urry, 2011). It is clear that, while we agree on many things, he is more pessimistic than I am on the supply of fossil fuels in the future, and he places more emphasis than I do on the impact of new information technologies. But the parallels between his social scenarios (ibid., p. 154) and mine are very strong. His Corbusier scenario (perpetual consumerism) is similar to my scenarios 1 and 2 above; his Schumacher scenario (local sustainability) is similar to my scenario 4; his Hobbesian scenario (regional warlordism) is similar to my scenario 5 (see below); and his digital scenario (low carbon, digital networks) is similar, in certain respects, to my scenario 3.

It has been difficult to specify the nature of the economic system 20 and 50 years hence, but confidence in the continuation of the slow shift in the underlying macro-geography of wealth and power, favouring East Asia at the expense of Europe and North America, seems well founded. The break up of China, an event that has occurred many times in that country's long history, is surely the only basis on which one might question such an expectation. If Japan, as a near neighbour (and because of this, the first to be affected by the extraordinary growth of China) is chosen as a model for what is likely to happen in Europe and North America, it can be expected that there will be a long and painful adjustment; a stagnation or even significant reduction in UK living standards (partially already achieved in the UK through currency movements and by the failure of wages to match inflation), greater job insecurity, high levels of government debt, significant decline in asset values (notably land and property) and a negative investment environment. The effects of this on internal migration in the UK are likely to be felt in part through lower mobility rates in general, but also through the impact such a shift will have on the UK as a destination for international migration. As major East Asian cities become magnets for international migrants (Guangzhou, almost inconceivably, already has a community of 20 000 West Africans), fewer people will seek to settle in the UK, thereby altering the spatial patterns of job availability for UK job seekers.

Having said this, as long as the present macro-geography of wealth and poverty holds some sway over migration decisions, people will continue to leave the poorer countries of the developing world for the EU, including the UK, and London will figure in the career plans of skilled migrants, both international and internal.

To summarize, it seems difficult to imagine that the economic drivers of internal migration in the UK will become any less important in the future than they have been in the recent past. The spatial links between people and employment, despite new communication technologies, will not lessen; indeed, if, as seems likely, there will be a long period of economic stagnation or recession with job insecurity and falling incomes, and if, as seems certain, retirement age is extended towards 70 (and maybe beyond) and dependence on earned income increases, then the need to be resident close to places of job opportunity will continue to be of crucial importance for the vast majority of the population.

8.3   TRENDS IN THE SOCIAL/CULTURAL, DEMOGRAPHIC AND POLITICAL DRIVERS OF MIGRATION

It is a widely held view that demographic ageing is the principal social change that will be affecting societies like the UK over the next 20 or 50 years. It is certainly true that, for a period of time, due to the greater lon-gevity and lower birth rates that are already in the system, the proportion of over 65s will increase. But what does this mean? If all that happens is that life courses are slightly slower to pan out, so that one stays in formal education a little longer and enters the workforce later, leaves the paren-tal home and sets up an independent household later, has children later, possibly starts a second family later and retires later, nothing much will have changed, socially or economically (but see Hollywood et al., 2007). Institutional and regulatory systems (such as pension entitlements) are already adjusting to these new realities. Furthermore, anxieties about the 'burden' of an older population on the health services are partially undermined by the argument that the costs of treatment of near-to-death patients do not differ greatly whether the person is aged 10, 50 or 90. It is very significant in this regard that 'adult disability dependency ratios' for the UK (that is, the ratio of adults with disabilities to those without them) are expected to remain exactly the same at 0.10 in the period from 2005–10 to 2045–50 (Sanderson and Scherbov, 2010).

Are there migration effects of these life course trends? Yes, the post-ponement of entry into work, and above all, the delay in a decision to marry or form a stable partnership and start a family, is partially choking off the flow of middle-class migrants from inner city locations to the city's suburbs and peri-urban districts. One can see some of the effects of this in the counter-ageing trend of certain Inner London and university city loca-tions (see Blake, 2009). Furthermore, the postponement of entry into work results in later achievement of a level of income needed to support home ownership – a problem that is made worse by the need to pay off debts incurred in obtaining a university education (Berrington et al., 2009). And the delay in family formation reduces the need for more household space. This results in an embedding of young middle-class professionals and managers in the inner city (at the expense, of course, of working-class households), which then fuels the gentrification process (Boddy, 2007). And every time a former area of working-class housing begins to be gentrified, it makes in-migration there and nearby easier for middle-class newcomers. They can now attach themselves to people and places that match their (student-formed) values and lifestyles, and, if financially able to do so (for example, through inheritance), they can purchase housing in areas that are undergoing improvement, that is, in areas where their investment in property is likely to be safe.

So, will this embourgeoisement of the inner city continue over the next 20 or 50 years? The answer is probably not. The proportion of 18-year-olds going into higher education in the UK seems unlikely to go much higher, and, due to funding changes, may well come down. The ratio of house prices to incomes is at a historical high and is likely to come down, making it easier to gain entry into home ownership. The historically low rates of house building probably will not last, especially as it is likely that, for some years to come, there will be a desperate need to boost domestic demand, for which purpose a major house-building programme is ideal (something that politicians from both main political parties seem to have been slow to recognize). And, finally, the decline in the fertility rate seems to have bottomed out. The implications of this for internal migration are that, in any of the four economic scenarios discussed above, the rates of suburbanization and peri-urbanization are fairly likely to increase.

Trends in the social class composition of the UK and in class-specific migration rates may, however, work in the other directions. In the case of scenario 1 (the continuation of neo-liberal globalization), social class polarization would result in:

- a small increase in the proportion of the very wealthy and power-ful, whose migration (or rather peripatetic lifestyles) would also increase, not only to maximize luxury consumption, but also for tax avoidance and other wealth protection purposes;
- increases in managers and white-collar workers, though probably not in their migrations;
- stability in proportions and migration rates of professionals and the petty bourgeoisie; and
- large decreases in the blue-collar workforce, and increases in the unemployed, due to a further hollowing out of the economy; this would in both cases, however, increase their migrations, because they would lose their entitlements to social housing and to social welfare support.

For scenario 2 (the transition towards a production-oriented form of capitalism), class inequality would certainly remain high, but the proportions in each class would be expected to change as would their class-specific migration rates:

- the proportions of managers and professionals would increase, though not their migration rates;
- the proportion of the very wealthy and powerful, the petty bourgeoisie and white-collar workers would decline, but without change in their migration rates;
- the big change would be for blue-collar workers, where both their proportion and migration rates would increase sharply; and
- the unemployed would decrease, but their migration rates would increase.

In the case of scenario 3 (the transition to social market capitalism), the results of a combination of an interventionist state and institutionalized collectivism would probably be:

- a decline in the proportion of the very wealthy and powerful, and managers, but no change in their migration rates;
- a sharp increase in professionals, and an increase in white-collar and blue-collar workers, but stability or decline in their migration rates;
- a decline in the petty bourgeoisie, and in the unemployed, and a decline also in the migration of the unemployed.

Finally, for scenario 4 (the transition to local socialism), the expected outcomes would be:

- a sharp decline in the size of the small group of very wealthy and powerful people, plus an end to their peripatetic lifestyles;
- a sharp decline in the proportion of managers, and perhaps also a decline in professionals and white-collar workers, with decreases in their migration rates;
- a sharp increase in blue-collar workers and an increase in the petty bourgeoisie, with a continuation, in both cases, of their low migration rates; and
- a sharp decline in the unemployed and a decrease in their migration.

Needless to say, it is extraordinarily difficult to anticipate changes in social structures and relations over a 20- or 50-year period within complex societies such as the UK. The reasons for this include the fact that we are talking about power relations produced by struggles between competing groups, each one using different strategies to achieve their goals, the outcomes from which are highly uncertain. But please note that in all cases discussed above other than scenario 1 (the continuation of neo-liberal globalization), there will probably be a reversal of the decline in the proportion of the workforce who belong to the manual working class. Other things being equal, this would imply a trend towards lower overall migration rates. Furthermore, there are signs of a tendency for the degree of autonomy in many professional and managerial jobs to decrease (although this would not be so under scenario 4), and this might also reduce spatial mobility because employer–employee relations for these middle classes would come to resemble those of the white-collar working class (for example, in having shorter career paths).

This brings the discussion to perhaps its most difficult task of all – to anticipate the role of culture/ethnicity as a migration driver in the future. We know (a) that there has been a significant convergence of occupational class structures between immigrant minorities and the host population in the past, both for first-generation migrants, but even more so for sub-sequent generations (Fielding, 2007); and (b) that the stigmatization of members of ethnic minorities is least where their presence in the popula-tion is greatest (and especially so in the case of London). These are the welcome signs of a progressive and respectful integration of minority cultures and ethnicities within the broader, shifting and multi-faceted stream of UK national culture. But it would be foolish to ignore three inter-related processes that point in a very different direction.

The first is the collapse of the multi-party and intellectual elite consen-sus around multiculturalism as a political goal or ideal, most notably in those countries that had previously built up very strong reputations for progressive forms of integration (such as the Netherlands and Denmark). Signs of this collapse are also now visible in the UK.

Second, economic decline, manifested especially in high unemployment and unaffordable housing, is underpinning the rise of a white 'backlash' working-class activism that has distinct racist, extreme nationalist, popu-list, anti-Islamic and neo-fascist overtones. Perhaps this is most clearly visible in the United States, where it seems not impossible that there will be a 'tea party' takeover of American right-wing politics. Such a development is also well advanced in several EU countries, and is represented in part by the rise of the English Defence League in the UK.

Finally, there is the issue of 'parallel lives' – the possibility that far from an integration of minority peoples and cultures with a mainstream UK culture that is simultaneously adjusting to diversity, the country will 'sleepwalk into segregation' – a recipe, many would say, for future confrontation and conflict (but see Stillwell and Duke-Williams, 2005; Hussain and Stillwell, 2008; Stillwell et al., 2008; Finney and Simpson,

2009; Simpson and Finney, 2009; Stillwell, 2010; Stillwell and Hussain, 2010). Were such a darker picture to become reality, which could be visualized as scenario 5 – a political economy characterized by an authoritarian regime sustained by, and promoting, extreme nationalism – there would be a major impetus to both micro-scale (for example, gated communities) and macro-scale ('white flight') resettlements of vast numbers of people as cultural/ethnic un-mixing took place. The migrations associated with such a 'securitization' of UK cities and countryside could be very substantial.

8.4   TRENDS IN THE ENVIRONMENTAL DRIVERS OF MIGRATION

At the overlap of the planning and architecture literature on the one hand and the energy security literature on the other, there is concern for the urban and rural settlement implications of 'peak oil' – that is, the point at which the rising curve of hydrocarbon production turns downwards due to a combination of resource scarcity and exorbitant development costs (Bridge, 2010). Specifically, will the shortage, and high cost, of fuel mean that people will re-concentrate in urban areas so that they could benefit from district heating for their homes, for example, or switch to public transport to avoid the very high costs of driving a car (UK: Government Office for Science, 2010)? The answer is probably not. A combination of social adjustments to higher fuel costs and new technological improvements in the discovery, exploitation and use of hydrocarbons is likely to result in a continued use of (though not, as in the past, an almost total dependence upon) oil and gas in the period up to 2060. The recent very positive reappraisal of North Sea (and North East Atlantic) oil and gas resources tends to lend support to this line of argument.

8.5   TRENDS IN THE CHARACTERISTICS OF THE MIGRATION DECISION

We know, often from personal experience, but also from family stories, that migration from one place to another is nearly always a major event. Indeed, it is one of those events around which an individual's biography is built. Furthermore, the feelings associated with migration are typically complicated and the decision difficult to make. Migration tends to expose one's personality; it expresses one's loyalties and reveals one's values and attachments (often previously hidden). As a statement of one's world view, it is a quintessentially cultural event (Fielding, 1992c).

Will this change in the future? Will hyper-mobility dull the attachments between people and place and lessen the significance of migration in people's lives? The answer is almost certainly not. In fact, it is largely a myth that we now live in a hyper-mobile society in the UK. Despite shifts in the social class composition of the UK population towards high-mobility groups, most age-specific inter-regional migration rates have either remained stable or decreased since the peak values of the late 1960s/early 1970s, and intra-regional migration rates, even during periods of house price booms, have never regained the high values reached during the period of post-World War II slum clearance and new town construction. The UK is, in many respects (and especially in comparison with the United States), a remarkably immobile society.

So the difficult decisions that dual-career households face, the reluctant substitutions of long-distance commuting for migration, and the tough decisions to 'live apart together' will continue to be made in the future. Yes, of course, new telecommunications technologies will make a difference. But the early predictions that home working would become the norm, and that the geographical link between workplace and residence would be irretrievably broken, have not turned out to be correct (except perhaps for a small group of self-employed IT specialists) (Daoust, 2010; but see Feldman, 2002). Migration, with all its practical and emotional complexities, will continue to matter enormously in people's lives.

8.6   MODELLING FUTURE INTERNAL MIGRATION FLOWS

A simple way to envisage the future distribution of a country's population is to use a multi-regional demographic model (for examples of quantitative modelling applied to internal migration in general and in the UK, see Stillwell et al., 1986; Weidlich and Haag, 1988; Congdon, 1989, 2008; Congdon and Champion, 1989; Rees et al., 1989, 1992; Gordon, 1992; Plane and Rogerson, 1994; Van der Gaag et al., 2000; UK: Office of the Deputy Prime Minister, 2002; Pellegrini and Fotheringham, 2002; Rees, 2008; Willekens, 2008; Raymer and Giulietti, 2010). This 'Rogers model approach' (Rogers, 1968, 1995, 2007) takes the present populations of regions, divided by age and sex, (1) ages them; (2) applies standardized mortality rates to calculate survivor populations, (3) adds new births; and (4) migrates them, again divided by age and sex, to other regions in the system on the basis of current age-specific and sex-specific migration rates (for modelling exercises using this kind of approach for the UK see Boden et al., 1991). Would it be helpful to carry out such an exercise for this project? No, unless the modelling incorporates assumptions other than a continuation of present rates (as is being done in the DEMIFER (Demographic and Migratory Flows Affecting European Regions and Cities) project on climate change and population redistribution in the EU – see Rees et al., 2010), it would not. The reasons are obvious: current migration patterns reflect both (a) the unique circumstances of the boom and bust of the late 2000s; and (b) the more general circumstances of late neo-liberal globalization, with its extreme forms of financialization and rent-based profit-making. Since the former will only recur if the latter remains as the dominant political economy, which, as was explained above, seems unlikely, one would be very ill-advised to base regional migration forecasts for 20 or 50 years hence on these current rates. The exercise would produce some figures ('hard data'), but what would those figures mean? Insofar as they had any meaning at all, it would be to illuminate the recent past. It would, sadly, tell us nothing at all about the future.

8.7   CONCLUSIONS

A necessary first step towards thinking about internal migration patterns in the UK in 20 and 50 years from now is to consider a possible range of alternative political economies. Five socioeconomic scenarios were identified: continuation of neo-liberal globalization (considered possible, but unlikely); reversion to production-oriented capitalism (considered likely); move to social market capitalism (considered possible); transition to local socialism (considered unlikely); and regression to a neo-fascist ultra-nationalism (considered very unlikely). Migration patterns for each of these scenarios were then explored. It was concluded that no decrease in the importance of economic drivers of internal migration was to be expected. In the case of social drivers, the demographic ageing of the population was argued to be far less important than is generally thought, likely trends in class composition and class-specific migration rates were explored, and the migration effects of ethnic un-mixing, though considered to be highly unlikely, were imagined. The migration effects of reaching 'peak oil' were judged to be far less significant than popular discourses might suggest. And despite revolutionary changes in communications technologies, it was argued that there would be no reduction in the significance for the individual of the decision to migrate.

PART III

UK internal migration: impacts of environmental change

9. Impacts of environmental change on UK internal migration

9.1 INTRODUCTION

There is a rapidly growing literature on climate change and on social adaptations to it (for useful general references see Lu et al., 2001; Haines et al., 2006; Dow and Downing, 2007; Dowling, 2007; O'Brien et al., 2008; Schipper and Burton, 2008; Stern, 2008; ESRC, 2009; Gemenne, 2009; Karl et al., 2009; Pittock, 2009; World Bank, 2009; Conway et al., 2010, Chapter 9; Harvey, 2010; Mearns and Norton, 2010; Moser, 2010; Shove, 2010; St Antony's International Review, 2010 (on the politics of climate change); UK: Government Office for Science, 2010).

However, while a fairly exhaustive bibliographic search has yielded a rich literature on the environmental change/migration nexus (Hugo, 1996, 2008; Myers, 1997; Black, 1998; Perch-Nielsen, 2004; Unruh et al., 2004; McLeman and Smit, 2006; Renaud et al., 2007; Adamo, 2008; Black et al., 2008, 2011; Boano et al., 2008; Brown, 2008; EU, 2008; Kniveton et al., 2008; Perch-Nielsen et al., 2008; Piguet, 2008, 2010a, 2010b; Raleigh et al., 2008; Barnett and Webber, 2009; IOM, 2009; Marchiori and Schumacher, 2009; McLeman, 2009, 2010; Morrissey, 2009; Reuveny and Moore, 2009; Tacoli, 2009; Warner et al., 2009; Afifi and Jager, 2010; Fritz, 2010; Fruhmann and Jager, 2010; Kalin, 2010; Laczko and Aghazarm, 2010; Martin, 2010; McAdam, 2010; McMichael et al., 2010; Raleigh and Jordan, 2010; Stephenson et al., 2010; Piguet and Picout, 2011; and see Lin, 2010 on the impact of environmental shocks on fertility, and Williams, 2008 on the legal status of climate-change-induced migrants), there were very few references on the sub-national impacts of climate change in the UK (and absolutely nothing on the impacts of climate change on internal migration). The partial exceptions to this generalization about sub-national impacts are: (1) the maps and key findings produced as part of the UKCP09 process, which show UK sub-national temperature, precipitation and sea level changes between now and future dates – one of which is the 2050s (UK: DEFRA, 2009); and (2) the regional integrated assessments of climate change impacts in East Anglia and North West England (Holman et al., 2005). Where such materials exist, they will, of course, be drawn upon in this chapter. But, in most cases, research on migration caused by environmental change relating to other parts of the world will be used to provoke thoughts about what might happen in the UK (the categories of environmental change used in this chapter are those employed by Raleigh et al., 2008). So the general format for the sub-sections that follow is: (a) a 'blue skies' speculation about the impact of a specific climate change on internal migration patterns; (b) an examination of research on the migration effects of such a climate change that might have relevance for the UK situation; and (c) conclusions, which take the form of how the former might require a rethinking, or at least modification, in the light of the latter.

9.2   THE ROLE OF DROUGHTS AND FAMINES

The location of the UK – its northern temperate latitude, surrounded by water bodies (Atlantic, North Sea, Irish Sea and English Channel), on the west side of a continental mass, in a zone of predominantly west winds – makes it extremely unlikely that drought will be a major problem resulting from climate change. Indeed, the middle estimates of the UKCP09 exercise (middle emissions, 50 per cent likelihood) suggest that annual precipitation levels in the 2050s will be approximately the same as they are now. That is not the whole story, however, since the same source suggests that summer precipitation levels may well be 10–30 per cent lower, and maybe even lower in the South West region. Lack of moisture in the growing season would affect agricultural yields of existing crops, and might lead to the cultivation of different crops, or to the more widespread use of irrigation. Southern Britain, however, is very fortunate in that there are major limestone aquifers for the storage of underground water – especially in the Cretaceous layer (chalk). So, even with longer dry spells and a higher use by agriculture for irrigation, it should be possible, though not necessarily easy, to manage water resources to maintain essential supplies to both urban and rural populations (but, if not, a national grid for water should solve the problem) (but see Arnell and Charlton, 2009).

If food shortages were to occur, they would be largely the product of failures in the supply chain, which, although possibly exacerbated by climate change both inside and outside the UK, would not be primarily due to this cause, but to disruptions caused by other serious economic or political problems. Furthermore, highly pessimistic views of the potential for food production in the UK should be dismissed; ever since the famous 'garden controversy' of the 1950s (when it was pointed out that houses with gardens containing vegetable plots produced as much or more food than the farmland that they replaced) (Best and Ward, 1956) we have real-ized that, with the investment of labour and technology, the potential food yield of UK land is extraordinarily high.

Although their social and physical characteristics are very different, can we learn something about the migration effects of droughts and famines in other countries that might be relevant to the UK? Yes, but the lessons are complex. For example, a key problem in developing countries is the very high dependence on agriculture, forestry and fishing for livelihoods. In contrast, only about 2 per cent of the UK workforce is in agriculture, so damage to the agricultural sector of the economy might be thought to have rather minimal economic significance. On the other hand, that 2 per cent produces about 60 per cent of UK food needs, so finding alternative sources at a time when food security was a major issue in other parts of the world would, almost certainly, prove to be problematic and very costly (Barling et al., 2008).

A study of northward migration from Mexican states into the United States estimates that a 10 per cent reduction in crop yields would lead an additional 2 per cent of the population to emigrate (Feng et al., 2010): 'by approximately the year 2080, climate change is estimated to induce 1.4 to 6.7 million adult Mexicans (or 2% to 10% of the current population aged 15–65) to emigrate as a result of declines in agricultural productiv-ity alone' (ibid., p. 14257) (for a similar study of drought-driven migra-tion in North East Brazil see Barbieri et al., 2010). Such drought-driven migrations are likely to be far less of a problem in UK agriculture (see above), but this study raises the intriguing possibility that there may be a reappraisal of agricultural land use within the UK, and that southern and south-eastern locations previously favoured for temperate cereals and live-stock production might give way to more Mediterranean-style cereals and fruit/vegetable production (Berry et al., 2006), while northerly locations, where summer high temperatures and water shortages may be less of a problem, might see a growth in agricultural land use and a switch towards increased livestock and temperate cereal production (Holman et al., 2005; Rounsevell and Reay, 2009).

A study of the social and environmental drivers of inter-provincial migration in Burkina Faso, West Africa (Henry et al., 2003) found that, despite there being an extraordinarily high dependence on agriculture, and the country being located in a climatically very marginal region (subject to Sahelian drought), 'the contribution of environmental variables in the explanation of migration was slightly lower than for the socio-economic variables' (ibid., p. 115). The key environmental drivers of out-migration were high rainfall variability, land degradation and poor land availabil-ity, that is, just those problems predicted to accompany climate change.

However, the lesson for internal migration in the UK is surely, that, if climatic problems are relatively unimportant in a country that is so vulnerable due to its poverty, dependence on agriculture and extremely high risk location, then such problems are unlikely to be major drivers of internal migration in a country like the UK that is far wealthier, has an urban-industrial economy and is located in a highly favourable low-risk location.

9.3   THE ROLE OF FLOODS AND LANDSLIDES

The UK is highly fortunate in its geomorphology as well as its climatic location. Yes, there is a long history of flood damage, but, due to the configuration of the country, that flooding tends to be very localized and very short-lived. This is because (1) the river basins are generally small; (2) the rivers are relatively short; (3) the slopes are generally gentle; and (4) many of the rocks, especially in the more populated parts of the country, are permeable. Geology also affects landslide risk; in upland UK, the rocks are very old, and generally hard and stable; in lowland UK, they are older, well-compacted sedimentary rocks that are also very largely stable. So it might be thought that the UK is well placed to come safely through the onset of both wetter winters and heavier precipitation in intensive bursts of bad weather.

The arguments set out above about the detrimental effects on agriculture of drought, and the related risk to food supplies, also apply to flooding. The impact on the economy, and the number of jobs adversely affected by the flooding of agricultural land would be expected to be very small, but the impact on food supplies could be considerable. However, in the case of flooding, other problems arise, notably (1) damage to transport, public service and utilities infrastructures, resulting in breaks of service; (2) damage to industrial and commercial property, resulting in losses of production and sales; (3) damage to people's homes, and disruption (sometimes even risk) to their lives; and (4) enhanced risk of disease. It is an unfortunate fact that many factories, utilities, shopping centres and housing estates have been built on river flood plains where they are now to some extent, and in the future probably to a much greater extent, vulnerable to flood damage (Wheater and Evans, 2009; UK: Government Office for Science, 2010, p. 21). So the (mostly local) migration and resettlement effects of increased flooding could be very significant.

Unlike the previous topic, in the case of floods and landslides we do have some material that discusses the regional impacts of climate change in the UK. The study entitled *Future Flooding* (UK: Office for Science and Technology, 2004; see also Wheater and Evans, 2009) sets out four different scenarios for future flooding in the UK. It points out that, except in the cases of 'local stewardship' (which looks a little like the 'local socialism' discussed above) and 'global sustainability' (which post-Copenhagen looks like a pipe dream; see Castles, 2010: 'adaptation is now the only game in town' p. 240), flood damage will considerably increase over the next 50 years. They also map the damage to show how the losses would be concentrated in certain coastal areas (see below) and in specific river basins such as the Yorkshire Ouse and the Thames. They argue that climate change will result in greater urban flooding, where unabsorbed run-off from heavy rainfall will exceed the capacity of urban sewerage and drainage systems to cope, resulting in a fourfold increase in the number of people at high risk. Finally, and more generally, under their 'world markets' scenario (which is like the 'neo-liberal' and 'production-oriented' capitalisms discussed above) they predict a rough doubling (from 1.6 million to 3.3 million) by the 2050s of the numbers of people at high risk from river and coastal flooding combined. Since serious flooding has occurred in the last ten years in (1) steep, narrow valley locations in western UK (Boscastle, Cornwall in 2004 (see Jennings, 2009), and Cumbria in 2010); (2) flood plains of major rivers in lowland UK (Don and Upper Thames Valleys in 2007, Tewkesbury in 2007); (3) river estuaries (Hull in 2007); and (4) gap towns where narrow outlets serve interior river basins (Lewes in 2000), it is very surprising that planning permissions are still being granted for developments in such locations. And with such low new build rates in the UK, the adjustment of the settlement pattern to increased flood risk is sure, at least in the near future, to be extremely slow. That such an adjustment to flood risk will, however, eventually take place is certain. Those who live in high-risk areas will find it difficult, costly or impossible to insure against flood damage (viz. the insurance companies paid out about £3 billion for the summer 2007 floods; RMS, 2007) and consequently the values of their properties will fall. They, themselves, may be unable to sell, and thereby become trapped in their current locations. But new entrants into the housing market and the very many who are relocating within owner occupation will come to realize that they must avoid high-flood-risk locations, and they will migrate instead to places that have a low or near-zero risk of flooding.

Are there lessons for internal migration in the UK to be found in research on climate-change-induced flooding in developing countries? Yes, perhaps rather surprisingly so. A study of climate change and migration in Bangladesh argues that migration is 'an important adaptive strategy for large sections of society in coping with climate-induced environmental degradation' (Sharma and Hugo, 2009, p. 1). They distinguish between gradual environmental change risks such as sea level rise and drought or desertification, and sudden environmental hazard risks such as cyclones and storm surges, floods and landslides, but point out that in both cases 'climate change migration' is mostly restricted to displacement within national boundaries, and that those who migrate tend to be the ones with the most developed and spatially extended social networks (viz. Chapter 4, Section 4.2). But the main lessons of this study for the UK are (1) the likelihood that there is, in general, an inverse relationship between the quality of governance and the importance of climate change as a driver of internal migration – the flood damage suffering and displacement in Bangladesh are very considerably due to the 'weak structures of governance' in that country – so any weakening of such structures in the UK, as a result, for example, of a political crisis, would result in a higher salience of climate change as a driver of internal migration; and (2) the inevitability that it will be those who are least able to cope with flood risk who will be both most likely to be exposed to it and most likely to suffer its migration consequences (see also Massey et al., 2010). We should remind ourselves that the 2007 floods in the UK were worst in Hull, but that insurance payouts per house flooded there were far less than elsewhere, because (a) the values of the properties and their contents were so much less there than in Gloucestershire and Oxfordshire, and (b) that many of the victims were un- or inadequately insured (RMS, 2007; for an interesting account of the flooding/sea level rise impacts on migration see Perch-Nielsen et al., 2008).

9.4   THE ROLE OF CYCLONES, WINDSTORMS AND WAVES

The UK is located, relative to other parts of the world, in a high wind zone; strong winds are experienced in a broad west–east belt extending from northern Spain to southern Scandinavia, but the strongest winds and most frequent windstorms are found in the British Isles, western France and the countries bordering the southern North Sea. However, since UK society is well adjusted to high winds, for example, through the kinds of houses that we live in, could it not be argued that any expected increases in the severity and frequency of high wind events should not be a cause of great concern? Yes, but once again, the likelihood is that certain people in specific environments will bear the brunt of climate change. The risks to lives and livelihoods through strong winds and high waves will be experienced most notably by seafarers, but also by others who work in outdoor occupations, especially, of course, farmers who risk losing their crops through wind damage. The risks to people in their homes will be felt most acutely by those living in old, poor-quality and badly maintained properties. There are, it is true, distinct spatial patterns of fishing, farming and poor-quality housing, but it is hard to imagine that either the prospect of a higher incidence of storms or the actual experience of storm damage (unless it is on a hurricane-force scale) will alone cause these people to migrate to other regions of the UK.

There is, however, a possible exception to this generalization. Recent research suggests that climate change will result in a very distinctive geography of heightened storm activity: '[T]he strength of the extreme storms are expected to increase in a band across central Europe (southern UK, German bight, northern Germany, and into eastern Europe)' (Schwierz et al., 2010, p. 511). This is the very same area that experienced the storm surge of 1953, when heightened sea level, high tides and massive waves combined to breach sea defences along the North Sea coasts of England and Holland, leading to much destruction and loss of life. When it is realized that this is the area that is also likely to be most adversely affected by a rise in sea level (see below), an abandonment of many low-lying coastal areas and a migration of people, probably mostly fairly locally to inland areas of eastern England, seems likely (see Nicholson-Cole and O'Riordon, 2009).

Searching outside the UK for lessons about the migration effects of a rise in the incidence of cyclones, one needs look no further than the growing literature on Hurricane Katrina (Gemenne, 2010). The migration effects of such severe weather events are both short term, due to property damage and the life-threatening danger of staying put, and long term, due in part to the understandable reluctance of people to return to such a high-risk location. In the City of New Orleans 385 000 people, out of a total population of 480 000, evacuated when Katrina made landfall in 2005. But nearly five years later in June 2009, the number of households in the City of New Orleans was still 23 per cent lower than the July 2005 estimate (figures taken from Gutmann and Field, 2010):

> The experience of (US hurricanes) suggests that the localization of the physical destruction of homes largely drives dislocation, which is strongly influenced by socio-economic and race-ethnic factors. Risk is not evenly distributed across society and those who are relatively privileged before a disaster have a greater diversity of options when facing calamity and a deeper well of resources to draw upon in the aftermath. The speed of reconstruction is also an important determinant of the return of out-migrants from a calamity, with slow reconstruction deferring return, and deferred returns eventually becoming permanent out-migration. (Gutmann and Field, 2010, p. 7)

These comments help us to think about the migration effects of almost any sudden highly localized calamity occurring in an advanced capitalist country, including the UK.

9.5   THE ROLE OF A RISE IN TEMPERATURE AND OF EXTREME TEMPERATURES

The UK's location in the cool temperate zone on the western maritime margin of the vast Eurasian continent ensures that extreme temperatures (for example, those outside the range −15°C to +35°C) are normally infrequent and short-lived. Global climate models suggest, however, that this will not continue to be the case in future (UKCP09). In addition to a 1–3°C increase in annual average temperature by the 2050s, there will be more extreme temperature events, not periods of unusually cold weather (which *should* decrease), but of unusually hot weather. And, from recent experience – the heatwave in the summer of 2003, when nearly 30 000 excess deaths occurred in Western Europe (with over 2000 in the UK) – we know that periods of unusually high temperatures are life-threatening (Haines et al., 2006). How might this impact on internal migration? Maybe it would reduce somewhat the attractiveness of southern regions over northern ones. But the main effect (plus perhaps an increase in fire risk) is more likely to be the further encouragement of migration from major cities to the countryside; this is because the 'heat island' effect makes cities even hotter than their surrounding areas (Lancet/UCL, 2009, p. 1702).

Very relevant to this discussion is a study of trends in cold- and heat-related mortality in England and Wales (Christidis et al., 2010; but see also Wolf et al., 2009). They show that the decline in cold-related mortality is much greater than the increase in heat-related mortality. Three key drivers of these trends are identified: human activity, climate change and adaptation. In the absence of adaptation, anthropogenic climate change would have been the main influence on these trends, but they found that adaptation was, in fact, even more important; it has prevented a significant increase in heat-related mortality, and greatly enhanced the decrease in cold-related mortality (on social adaptation to climate change see Adger et al., 2009a and b). This is very helpful when thinking about the effects of climate change on internal migration, because it warns us against assuming an unmediated relationship between the environment and human behaviour. In fact, what happens is that people tend to adjust to these kinds of challenges by changing their behaviour, and they tend to do so in situ, without migrating.

A further interesting perspective on cold-related mortality is provided by a study that examines the effects of migration from regions that experience severe cold weather to regions that are much warmer. The researchers found that 'longevity gains associated with mobility from the Northeast (USA) to the Southwest account for 4% to 7% of the total gains in life expectancy experienced by the U.S. population over the past thirty years' (Deschenes and Moretti, 2009, p. 659). This link between migration and longevity reminds us that Europe also has its 'snowbird' migrations, where some Northern Europeans, including UK citizens, spend their whole retirements, or sometimes just their winter months, in the Mediterranean south. The temperature increases associated with anthropogenic climate change might reduce the popularity of such long-distance migrations, and could conceivably result in the substitution of internal migration for international migration while maintaining the (albeit small) longevity gains.

9.6   THE ROLE OF A RISE IN SEA LEVEL

The UK is fortunate (for the fifth time!) in not having those landscape features that would make it particularly vulnerable to sea level rise. There are no vast lowlands, no deltas, and only a small number of areas of extensive, reclaimed, low-lying marshland (the Fens, Somerset Levels, Romney Marsh, etc.). Furthermore, the UKCP09 central estimates for sea level rise (2060 compared with 1990) are fairly moderate, ranging from 26 cm for London and Cardiff to 17 cm for Edinburgh. The problem is that only modest rises in sea level can make two other problems much worse: the first is river flooding – the combination of heavy rainfall, high tides and sea level rise would be likely to exacerbate flood damage in the lower reaches of the UK's largest rivers; the second is coastal flooding – the combination of deep cyclonic weather, high tides, waves and sea level rise would be likely to exacerbate flood damage along the coasts of the UK, especially perhaps down the east coast. Furthermore, it is obviously the case that most of the UK's largest cities are coastal, and that land at, or close to, sea level is typically very intensively used. However, the wilder speculations about the flooding of London and other large towns and cities must be firmly rejected (Environment Agency, 2009). So immensely valuable are the low-lying parts of these cities that the owners have a strong vested interest in their protection from flooding. Of course, this flood protection is much more difficult to achieve in an individualistic, small-state, market-oriented economic system than in a mixed-economy, large-state, planning-oriented one. But, by one route or another, we can be confident, almost certain, that powerful agents protecting extremely valuable property assets will ensure that investment in urban flood prevention will be undertaken. What happens in rural flood plains and coastal areas is another matter.

It follows, therefore, that we should not expect a mass evacuation of

UK cities over the next 50 years as businesses and households try to escape the effects of sea level rise. Instead, we should expect flood prevention investments, some of them prompted after the event of serious flooding rather than anticipating it, to be made in urban areas (Nicholls, 2003; Hallegatte et al., 2008; Nicholls et al., 2008; Reeder et al., 2009). But, at the same time, there will almost certainly be some abandonment of the least valuable low-lying coastal land, where the costs of flood prevention are judged to be greater than the benefits of flood protection.

Empirical studies tend to support the generalizations made above. A study of the world's low elevation coastal zones (LECZs) points out that while only 2 per cent of the land area of the world is below 10 m, this area accounts for 10 per cent of world population, and 13 per cent of the urban population (McGranahan et al., 2007). What is more, the population of this zone is increasing rapidly as urbanization proceeds. No European country, however, figures in the top 20 countries for the absolute size of their populations in LECZs, and only one figures for the percentage of their populations in LECZs (Netherlands third at 74 per cent), thus confirming the relative advantage of the UK. They also report that 'in the absence of any other changes, a sea level rise of 38 centimetres would increase five-fold the number of people flooded by storm surges' (ibid., p. 20).

This brings us to a study of the social impact of sea level rise in an area subject to hurricanes, Sarasota County, Florida (Frazier et al., 2010). The most significant result of their research was to show that the effect of a 1.2 m rise in sea level was equivalent to raising the storm severity by one category in the five-category Saffir–Simpson Hurricane Wind Scale. In other words, it very significantly increased the likely damage, and the spatial extent of the area flooded. The message from these studies is clear; insofar as there are migration effects of sea level rise in the UK, they will be most acutely felt in those fairly restricted areas where (1) there are no new flood defences, and (2) where sea level rise combines with other hazards such as storm surges to cause serious river flood plain and coastal flooding.

9.7 THE ROLE OF ALTERED CONDITIONS FOR THE SPREAD OF DISEASE

Changes in the spatial flows of people and goods accompanying globalization have altered the susceptibility of populations to the spread of disease, so that, to take one example, pandemics of genetically new forms of influenza (such as human versions of 'bird flu' and 'swine flu') have become a real health threat. But this has nothing to do with climate change (Lancet/ UCL, 2009, p. 1703). The specific threat posed by climate change to countries in high latitudes is that diseases that are now endemic to tropical or sub-tropical regions will spread northwards (or southwards in the case of the southern hemisphere) towards previously disease-free temperate regions. Undoubtedly, mosquito-borne diseases, notably malaria, but also dengue fever, pose the greatest risk, this risk being all the greater because people in these regions lack immunity to the diseases (ibid., p. 1702). Some experts disagree in the case of malaria (see Gething et al., 2010). They point out that, despite a century of warming, there has been a marked decline in malaria and a substantial weakening of the correlation between malaria endemicity and climate. In contrast, the threat from dengue fever is considered likely to increase. This is due to the lack, at present, of successful forms of prevention and treatment, and the fact that, unlike malaria, dengue is just as prevalent in urban districts as in rural areas (Jasparro and Taylor, 2008, p. 249). 'By 2080 about 6 billion people will be at risk of contracting dengue fever (with) climate change, compared with 3.5 billion people if the climate remained unchanged' (Lancet/UCL, 2009, p. 1703). The UK, however, is well outside the regions that are most at risk of becoming areas where these diseases are endemic:

> Health authorities need to remain alert to the possibility of future European malaria outbreaks or to the arrival in the UK of better European vectors (carriers) of malaria. Any malaria outbreaks in the UK, however, are likely to be rare and on a small scale, involving a small number of people. Prompt reaction to any outbreaks will reduce the chances of endemic malaria transmission in the UK. (UK: Department of Health, 2008, p. 34)

Should these prompt reactions fail, and a localized outbreak of a life-threatening disease such as malaria occur, resulting not from travellers returning to the UK, but from local transmission of the disease, it is possible that a large temporary migration away from that area would ensue (as happened in China when migrants to the Guangdong region returned to their inland rural origins during the SARS outbreak in 2003). This might endanger others, of course, because the migrant might be carrying the disease to new areas. To avoid this, the authorities would be likely to impose strict quarantine measures. But, as has been pointed out (Mesnard and Seabright, 2009, p. 933), 'overall disease prevalence may even increase if, in the name of avoiding negative externalities (by restricting migration), the authorities discourage relatively low-risk individuals from escaping the epicenter of the disease, thereby increasing the probability that they will catch the disease there from infected individuals'.

To summarize, assuming rapid response and good governance, there should be no major internal migration flows in the UK, either permanent or temporary, resulting from climate-induced changes in the patterns of disease (Wilkinson, 2006).

9.8   THE INDIRECT ROLE OF ENVIRONMENTAL CHANGE (FOR EXAMPLE, THROUGH SOCIAL CONFLICT)

The television drama called 'The March' (shown by the BBC in 1990, directed by David Wheatley, written by William Nicholson) is a fictional account (but not regarded in some circles as a particularly far-fetched one; see Christian Aid, 2007) of climate-change-induced migration from Africa (Sudan) to Europe (Spain). The migrants, led by a charismatic leader called Isa El-Mahdi, suffer attacks from armed gangs as they cross Sudan (is it Darfur?), lose many through starvation and dehydration in the Sahara, gain many more migrants as they travel and eventually reach Tangiers 250 000 strong. They cross the Straits of Gibraltar to face European military forces blocking their way. The story ends enigmatically with a media-recorded stand-off between penniless migrants on one side and the armed defenders of European borders (and of the privileged lives of those who live within them) on the other. The storyline is just about believable and the dialogue is sometimes quite perceptive (as when the Irish EU Commissioner for Development, played by Juliet Stevenson, is trying to educate her fellow Commissioners about the political realities of climate-induced migration). But is there a lesson here for internal migration in the UK? The answer is probably not. The inequalities within the UK are not now, or likely to be in the future, of the same order as those between Africa and the EU. No one, surely, would block or confront counter-urban migrants, or migrants from the core to the periphery who might conceivably be migrating because of processes related to climate change. And yet, having said that, we would be wise to remember the massive anti-urban-dweller prejudices of many of the supporters of the Countryside Alliance, and perhaps also the reported 'Sons of Glyndwr' campaign of the 1980s to firebomb English-owned second homes in rural Wales and English estate agents' premises dealing in Welsh property (Green, 1992b; see also Walford, 2004; Day et al., 2010). And perhaps we should also consider what immigration policy Scotland would adopt if it became an independent nation outside the EU (see Graham and Boyle, 2003 and Wilson and Rees, 2003 on population policy and Scottish devolution). 'The reality may be that adaptation to climate risks may be punctuated, messy, more costly than we are willing to pay, and be at odds with legitimate values and strongly held conviction concerning place and identity' (Adger and Barnett, 2009, p. 2804).

Looking outside the UK, one author claims to show that half of the 38 major 'environmental migrations' over the last 50 years or so resulted in violent conflict (Reuveny, 2007). He argues that:

> [W]hereas developed economies can absorb migrants in various sectors, under-developed economies, reliant on the environment for survival, are limited in this regard, particularly if their resources are scarce. Therefore they are more prone to conflict due to the arrival of environmental migrants. (Ibid., p. 659)

But then he goes on to state more generally:

> [W]hen migration flows are small and slow, migrants can be absorbed more smoothly, lessening the likelihood of conflict. Thus far, climate change has induced slow changes, but its effects are expected to include evermore frequent and intense droughts and storms. Quick changes of this type can push many to migrate quickly, especially when they depend on the environment for liveli-hood. In this case, the forces promoting conflict in the receiving area may be stronger. (Ibid., p. 660)

Echoing the theme of 'The March', he concludes by writing:

> [F]acing growing migration pressures of Less Developed Countries, the Developed Countries have made immigration from LDCs more difficult. I believe this approach will likely become less effective as climate change contin-ues, facing ever-rising environmental migration pressures. (Ibid., p. 668)

(For a contrary view that locates climate-induced migration within devel-oping countries see Barnett and Webber, 2010.) Is this relevant to the UK? Yes, as has been discussed above, any sizeable increase in immigration to the UK would be likely to impact upon patterns of internal migration, probably in counter-urban and core-to-periphery directions.

9.9   CONCLUSIONS

This chapter has searched widely for material relevant to anticipating the impacts on internal migration in the UK of environmental change over the next 20 and 50 years. The main conclusions are as follows:

1. The UK is extremely well placed, perhaps even uniquely well placed, to adjust to climate change without a major redistribution of its population.

2. A minor qualification of this is that greater river and coastal flooding will make some areas hazardous for settlement – planning permissions for urban development in such areas should stop right now.
3. The key factor affecting adjustment to climate change is the quality and responsiveness of government. It follows that this is hardly the best time to be experimenting with a political economy (neo-liberal globalization) that is wholly dependent on market-based solutions to pressing social and environmental problems.

10. Implications for policy

10.1 INTRODUCTION

This final chapter connects what has been discussed in Chapter 9 to two policy arenas – the national and the international. It begins by classifying the migration outcomes outlined there using the distinction between (1) outcomes that were expected to be relatively slow, and unforced, involving gradual shifts in population, which we shall call 'mobility'; and (2) outcomes that were expected to be rapid, sudden and typically forced or at least occurred as a matter of last resort, which we shall call 'displacement'. Each of these will then be sub-divided on the basis of whether the policy challenges are thought to be primarily technical/managerial or primarily political.

10.2 MOBILITY THAT POSES 'TECHNICAL' OR MANAGERIAL CHALLENGES

The research and reasoning used in Chapter 9 above produced no strong expectations that environmental change would result in major shifts in the distribution of the UK population by means of 'routine' mobility. Migration patterns will evolve, but the driving forces will, almost totally, be economic, social and political, not environmental. The minor exceptions are:

- Small-scale migrations associated with shifts in agriculture, forestry and fishing that might reflect adjustments to dry summers, higher temperatures and the availability of irrigation (Section 9.2).
- Local migrations associated with the avoidance of flood risk from both rivers and sea (9.3 and 9.6). This would mostly affect flood plains of the major UK rivers and low-lying land in eastern coastal districts. Some abandonment of individual dwellings (for example, on east coast cliff tops) and small settlements located in areas of poor-quality agricultural land liable to flooding is to be expected.
- Very largely local migrations associated with the avoidance of very high temperatures in large city (heat island) locations (9.5).

10.3   MOBILITY THAT POSES POLITICAL CHALLENGES

No significant cases of political challenges posed by mobility were discussed in Chapter 9. Two messages, however, that might come under the this heading relate to: (1) the short-sighted behaviour of allowing development on land that, over the next 50 years, is increasingly likely to suffer a high risk of flooding (9.3 and 9.6); and (2) the need to consider climate change in any discussion of measures to be taken to avoid future food scarcity (9.2) (UK Government Office for Science, 2011, p. 12).

10.4   DISPLACEMENT THAT POSES TECHNICAL CHALLENGES

The research and reasoning used in Chapter 9 above produced no strong expectations that environmental change would result in major shifts in the distribution of the UK population by means of sudden displacements. The minor exceptions are:

- local temporary migrations associated with river and coastal flooding, which is expected to become increasingly severe and frequent (9.3 and 9.6);
- local temporary migrations associated with what will probably be very infrequent severe windstorms (9.4);
- mostly local temporary, but possibly also permanent migration, associated with storm surge damage arising from the combination of river flooding, high tides, windstorms, deep cyclonic weather, high waves and sea level rise (9.3, 9.4 and 9.6); and
- local and regional, mostly temporary, migrations associated with escape from the (very unlikely) outbreak of a life-threatening former tropical disease that has now become endemic in the UK (9.7).

10.5   DISPLACEMENT THAT POSES POLITICAL CHALLENGES

No significant cases of political challenges posed by displacement were discussed in Chapter 9. The minor cases were:

- the possibility, but only in highly charged political circumstances, of resistance to the migration of English people to the regions and countries of northern and western UK (Scotland, Wales, Northern Ireland and Cornwall) (9.8);

• the possibility of rural resistance to an influx of urban dwellers in similar circumstances (9.8); and

• the 'knock-on' effects on internal migration (likely to be counter-urban and core-to-periphery in direction) of the unlikely sudden arrival of very many 'climate change migrants' from outside the UK (9.8).

To conclude, this conceptual framework is judged to be valid and helpful, but probably more useful for the study of the outcomes of environmental change on international migration rather than internal migration.

10.6 INTERGOVERNMENTAL PANEL ON CLIMATE CHANGE SCENARIOS

The second part of this chapter addresses the relevance of IPCC (Intergovernmental Panel on Climate Change) emissions scenarios for a study of the likely impact of environmental change on internal migration in the UK (IPCC, 2000; see also IPCC, 2001, 2007).

The A1 scenario
The A1 storyline and scenario family describes a future world of very rapid economic growth, global population that peaks in mid-century and declines thereafter, and the rapid introduction of new and more efficient technologies. Major underlying themes are convergence among regions, capacity building, and increased cultural and social interactions, with a substantial reduction in regional differences in per capita income.

(IPCC, 2000, p. 4)

Ignoring its internal contradictions for a moment, one can perhaps view this scenario, thought up in the late 1990s, as the product of a historical moment – the 'end of history' euphoria that followed the US victory over the Soviet Union in the Cold War. Twelve years later it looks naive, almost foolish.

But if such a world existed in 2060, what would it imply for environmental migration within the UK? The answer is probably very little other than what has already been outlined in Chapter 9 above. I am not saying that it would have no impact on internal migration flows in the UK, only that it would have a minimal affect on climate-change-induced migration. Insofar as it seems to reject any mitigation of climate change, it might make the problems listed above a little more serious than would otherwise be the case. As a scenario it bears some resemblance to the scenario 1 (continuation of neo-liberal globalization) set out in Chapter 8, Section 8.2, but it is a version that is stripped of all that system's faults and weaknesses (its dangerous instability, its promotion of multiple gross anti-social behaviours, and its massive negative environmental externalities).

The A2 scenario

The A2 storyline and scenario family describes a very heterogeneous world. The underlying theme is self-reliance and preservation of local identities. Fertility patterns across regions converge very slowly, which results in continuously increasing global population. Economic development is primarily regionally oriented and per capita economic growth and technological change are more fragmented and slower than in other storylines.

(IPCC, 2000, p. 5).

It is hard to fathom what kind of society this scenario is envisaging, but it might be what in Chapter 8, Section 8.2, is identified as scenario 4 and called 'local socialism'. It is interesting that this is viewed as the scenario that does worst on the economic front, as though autonomy and mutuality were somehow less efficient than competition and interdependence. Once again, this partly reflects its datedness – the 'Washington Consensus' was in its ascendancy at that time, and the rise of China was still in its early stages.

But if such a world existed in 2060, what would it imply for environmental migration within the UK? The answer is probably very little, or rather very little apart from what has already been outlined in Chapter 9. I am most assuredly not saying, of course, that it would have no impact on internal migration flows in the UK, only that it is hard to envisage how it could affect climate-change-induced migration. Except, that is, that it might perhaps encourage a local mobilization of efforts to adapt to environmental change in ways that were less likely to damage the interests of the poor and the weak.

The B1 scenario

The B1 storyline and scenario family describes a convergent world with the same global population that peaks in mid-century and declines thereafter, as in the A1 storyline, but with rapid changes in economic structures toward a service and information economy, with reductions in material intensity, and the introduction of clean and resource-efficient technologies. The emphasis is on global solutions to economic, social, and environmental sustainability, including improved equity, but without additional climate initiatives.

(IPCC, 2000, p. 5)

Once again, internal contradictions abound (who grows the food, makes the machines, builds the houses?) – this is a make-believe world of astounding naivety, a kind of United Nations enthusiast's fantasy. It is not surprising perhaps that the word 'sustainability' (a word that has become, surely, almost devoid of meaning) makes its first appearance in this scenario.

But if such a world were to exist in 2060, what would it imply for environmental migration within the UK? The answer is probably nothing; nothing, that is, apart from what has already been outlined in Chapter 9. Once again, I am not saying that it would have no impact on internal migration flows in the UK, only that it would not affect climate-change-induced migration, unless, and this is crucial, it resulted in significant efforts being put into mitigation. As a scenario it bears some resemblance to the scenario 3 (emergence of social market capitalism) in Chapter 8, Section 8.2, except that it is global in scale and seemingly almost miraculously efficient at solving the world's social and environmental problems.

The B2 scenario

The B2 storyline and scenario family describes a world in which the emphasis is on local solutions to economic, social, and environmental sustainability. It is a world with continuously increasing global population at a rate lower than A2, intermediate levels of economic development, and less rapid and more diverse technological change than in the B1 and A1 storylines. While the scenario is also oriented toward environmental protection and social equity, it focuses on local and regional levels.

(IPCC, 2000, p. 5)

This has all the hallmarks of a watered-down version of A2. It is local/regional, concerned with social equity, and, as with A2, is inefficient, and lacks economic and technological dynamism. Whatever the claim about the neutrality of the scenarios, A2 and B2 are characterized by associations that are, in my judgement, intended to stigmatize them – high population growth, low technological innovation and poor GDP performance.

But if such a world existed in 2060, what would it imply for environmental migration within the UK? The answer is surely little or nothing, apart from what has already been outlined in Chapter 9. Please note that I am most assuredly not saying that it would have no impact on internal migration flows in the UK, only that it would not affect climate-change-induced migration. As a scenario it bears some resemblance to scenario 4 (local socialism) in Chapter, 8, Section 8.2, except that it is doubtful if any of the IPCC scenarios break away from a capitalist, private-ownership, profit-driven, market-based economy. What a courageous, or perhaps foolhardy, vote of confidence in the status quo that represents!

10.7   CONCLUSION

My highly critical comments in this part of the text reflect (1) my judgement that these IPCC scenario differences have almost no impact on the
environmental drivers of internal migration in the UK; and (2) my judgement that these scenarios were more than reasonably, or perhaps even
properly, influenced by the circumstances of that precise moment, 1998,
which saw their creation.

   So what needs to be done to improve the quality of the social science
thinking that goes into these scenario-building exercises? First, the population numbers and GDP growth obsessions of US trained economists
(manifested in the present IPCC scenarios) need to be tempered by har-
nessing the insights of other social scientific traditions, notably those
of sociologists and geographers, but above all, of those social scientists
who adopt a political economy approach. After all, it is these latter who
study the variety of social and economic systems that do and have existed,
and are best placed, therefore, to say useful things about the societies
that might exist in 20 and 50 years' time. Second, we need practical clas-
sifications of policy options, perhaps of the kind developed recently to
discuss EU climate change policy (Stripple et al., 2010). They identify
'four worlds': (1) coordinated mitigation ('Kyoto+++'); (2) autonomous
mitigation ('fragmentation and low-carbon competition'); (3) coordinated
adaptation ('sharing the burdens of adaptive planning'); and (4) autonomous adaptation ('let them adapt!'). Their expectations are that policy
interventions will be initially confined to those areas in which the EU
already has competence (e.g., agriculture, water and biodiversity protection) and will only be extended into new areas such as migration, land-use
planning and coastal defence if the impacts of climate change (floods,
storms, etc.) 'become so severe as to constitute a focusing event' (ibid.,
p. 239).

Conclusions

PART I

Chapters 2 and 3 described in considerable detail some of the important features of the internal migration flows in the United Kingdom at both regional/country and county levels for both the recent period (2009–10) and at the time of the last population Census (2000–01). Amongst many things, they showed the following:

1. The in- and out-migration rates for certain regions and counties are extraordinarily low while others are just as surprisingly high. The reasons for the low rates surely include geographical remoteness, the strength of cultural identity and population size, but in addition, as was shown later, the social class composition of the population seems to be absolutely crucial to an understanding of differences across counties in in- and out-migration rates. The fact that the gross in- and out-migration rates are strongly positively correlated (when economic logic suggests that they should be negatively related) represents a challenge to our understanding that was confronted in Part II.

2. London plays a central role in the UK migration system. It has a unique age-specific migration profile, and, despite being the pinnacle of wealth concentration, luxury consumption and celebrity success, has been shown to be a massive net loser by internal migration, except, most importantly, for young adults. This also called out for explanation.

3. The patterns of gains and losses and of the individual flows were found to be remarkably similar between the 2000–01 and 2009–10 dates. Where differences occurred, they fitted well with the notion that migration at the earlier date was reflecting buoyant employment and housing markets, whereas at the later date these employment and housing market forces were so powerfully subdued by recession as to project other patterns, notably those associated with student migrations, into prominence. Both the underlying stability and the changes over the economic cycle also called out for explanation. It is to these explanations for internal migration, or 'drivers' of migration, in the UK that we turned to in Part II.

163

PART II

Chapters 4 to 8 provide the following conclusions:

1. The economic drivers of internal migration in the UK are of para-mount importance. They typically imply migration for the purpose of gaining employment, or for improved terms and conditions in employment, and can be usefully grouped into (a) short-term business cycle processes; (b) medium-term restructuring processes; and (c) long-term 'deep structural' processes (such as the 'escalator region' character of the London/South East region) – and of these, the restructuring processes are particularly important (and probably the least well understood). In addition, it was shown that unemployment was far less of a driver of migration than would be expected on the basis of economic logic, and that housing was far more of a driver than expected. Student migrations were also emphasized because they had become so important in the recent period. Finally, it was pointed out that the spatial separation of the 'earning' of unearned income from the spending of it, boosted by the rising share of unearned income as a proportion of total income, helps to explain the high net in-migration gains of high-amenity areas (such as South West England), even when, as is often the case, the economic performance of these areas is poor.

2. The social, demographic and political drivers of internal migration in the UK are also very important indeed. There are striking differ-ences between social classes in their inter-regional migration rates. Furthermore, the link between migration and intra-generational social class mobility is particularly significant – those who move spa-tially tend also to succeed socially. Internal migration is also highly gendered, and there are strong links between migration, gender-specific social mobility rates and family formation behaviours. One of the key social drivers of migration is the individual's life course, with particular kinds of migration associated with each transition (for example, a suburban or peri-urban move linked to the enlargement of the family). Finally, culture and ethnicity are drivers of migration, with the same feature of a region (such as high cultural diversity) having differential effects on migration – encouraging some to move in, while encouraging others to move out.

3. Despite the importance granted in the literature to environmental drivers of internal migration in the UK, largely based upon the results of questionnaire surveys of migrants' reasons for moving, the judgement of this review was that environmental drivers are far

less important than social drivers, which in turn are less important than economic drivers. And finally, that difficult trade-offs between migration, commuting and circulation exist for many households, but perhaps especially so for dual-career households.

4. A necessary first step towards thinking about internal migration patterns in the UK in 20 and 50 years from now is to consider a possible range of alternative political economies. Five socioeconomic scenarios were identified: continuation of neo-liberal globalization (considered possible, but unlikely); reversion to production-oriented capitalism (considered likely); move to social market capitalism (considered possible); transition to local socialism (considered unlikely); and regression to a neo-fascist ultra-nationalism (considered very unlikely). Migration patterns for each of these scenarios were then explored. It was concluded that no decrease in the importance of economic drivers of internal migration was to be expected. In the case of social drivers, the demographic ageing of the population was argued to be far less important than is generally thought, likely trends in class composition and class-specific migration rates were explored, and the migration effects of ethnic un-mixing, though considered to be highly unlikely, were imagined. The migration effects of reaching 'peak oil' were judged to be far less significant than popular discourses might suggest. And despite revolutionary changes in communications technologies, it was argued that there would be no reduction in the significance for the individual of the decision to migrate.

PART III

From Chapters 9 and 10, the following conclusions may be drawn:

1. The impacts of environmental change on internal migration could be studied under seven headings: droughts and famines; floods and landslides; cyclones, windstorms and waves; rises in temperature and more temperature extremes; rise in sea level; altered conditions for the spread of disease; and effects of environmental change on social conflict. The effects of these changes on migration were considered to be probably relatively minor; the UK was judged to be extremely well placed to adjust to climate change without a major redistribution of its population. A minor exception to this is that greater river and coastal flooding is likely to render some areas hazardous to settlement and/or very costly to protect. And crucial to successful adaptation is good governance – a strong state that can plan and execute major

environmental infrastructures, and can respond quickly and decisively to environmental challenges.
2. That the migration outcomes of environmental change can be successfully classified into: mobility that poses technical or managerial challenges (minor); mobility that poses political challenges (non-existent); displacement that poses technical challenges (minor); and displacement that poses political challenges (minimal).
3. Finally, the conclusions of this study were matched to the four emissions scenarios developed for IPCC (2000). These scenarios were judged, however, to be very dated and almost irrelevant for the further consideration of the effects of environmental change on internal migration in the UK.

FINAL COMMENTS

The reader will probably have noticed two very important things: (1) that the impacts of environmental change discussed in Part III seemed, with one interesting exception, to be unaffected by the nature of the social scenarios discussed in Part II. The exception is the argument that adaptation to environmental change would be likely to be easier in a situation where the state had the authority and the resources to intervene decisively to ensure that necessary steps, such as flood protection infrastructure investments, were taken (rather than leaving matters to 'free' markets, which tend to be highly conservative, can be very inefficient, and are sometimes corrupted by nepotism and clientelism); and (2) that the possible migrations promoted by environmental change were insignificant (say perhaps in their tens of thousands over a decade) in comparison with those that were likely to accompany either a retention of the present system of neo-liberal globalization, or a shift to an alternative political economy. It should be remembered that in 2009–10 alone, roughly 2 million people migrated between counties/metropolitan cities in the UK. Putting it rather crudely, when it comes to internal migration, 'social-system-and-social-system-change', trumps 'environmental-drivers-and-environmental-change' every time.

This judgement links our topic to a much wider debate. There was a great fashion in the early twentieth century to ascribe the main events of early European history to the 'pulse of Asia'. This 'pulse' was activated by periodic drought in the 'heartland' of Central Asia. The argument melded well with the social Darwinism and environmental determinism of the time. Every time Central Asia experienced drought or some other environmental disaster, 'hordes' of nomadic tribespeople invaded the civilized, settled agricultural lands of the Euro-Asiatic periphery (Europe, South West, Southern and South East Asia and China). We now know this to be nonsense. The Mongols in the thirteenth century, for example, migrated not because they were prisoners of a hostile nature, but because, through superior social organization, they were the masters of their own environment, and of the peoples and environments around them. And if the 'pulse of Asia' was nonsense at a time when people depended on the natural environment far, far more than they do today, and when they had few technologies to mitigate environmental change or to make adjustments to it, then one should surely be extremely cautious about ascribing to 'environmental change' a key causal role in explaining human migration flows today, including, more specifically, the migrations to, from, and within the UK (in this matter I side with Black, 2001, Castles, 2002 and Raleigh and Jordan, 2010; see also Hartmann, 2010 on the politics of 'climate refugees'). In short, '(e)nvironmental change is never a sole cause of migration . . . there are always one or more underlying economic, political or other social factors that make environmental change a proximate trigger, rather than an underlying driver of migration' (O'Brien et al., 2008, p. 24).

References

Abreu, M., M. Kitson and P. Wales (2009), 'The movement of talent: migration patterns among UK graduates and implications for regional economic disparities', UK Innovation Research Centre, PowerPoint presentation.

Adamo, S. (2008), 'Addressing environmentally induced population displacements: a delicate task', available at: http://www.population environmentresearch.org; accessed 4 January 2012.

Adger, W.N. and J. Barnett (2009), 'Four reasons for concern about adaptation to climate change', *Environment and Planning A*, **41**(12), 2800–805.

Adger, W.N. et al. (2009a), 'Are there social limits to adaptation to climate change?', *Climatic Change*, **93**(3–4), 335–54.

Adger, W.N., I. Lorenzoni and K.L. O'Brien (eds) (2009b), *Adapting to Climate Change: Thresholds, Values, Governance*, Cambridge: Cambridge University Press.

Afifi, T. and J. Jager (eds) (2010), *Environment, Forced Migration and Social Vulnerability*, Heidelberg: Springer.

Arnell, N.W. and M.B. Charlton (2009), 'Adapting to the effects of climate change on water supply reliability', in W.N. Adger, I. Lorenzoni and K.L. O'Brien (eds), *Adapting to Climate Change: Thresholds, Values, Governance*, Cambridge: Cambridge University Press, pp. 42–53.

Barbieri, A.F. et al. (2010), 'Climate change and population migration in Brazil's Northeast: scenarios for 2025–2050', *Population and Environment*, **31**(5), 344–70.

Barker, K. (2004), *Review of Housing Supply: Delivering Stability: Securing Our Future Housing Needs*, London HM Treasury.

Barling, D., R. Sharpe and T. Lang (2008), 'Rethinking Britain's food security', a research report for the Soil Association, City University, London.

Barnett, J. and M. Webber (2009), *Accommodating Migration to Promote Adaptation to Climate Change*, Stockholm: Commission on Climate Change and Development.

Barnett, J. and M. Webber (2010), 'Migration as adaptation: opportunities and limits', in J. McAdam (ed.), *Climate Change and Displacement: Multidisciplinary Perspectives*, Oxford and Portland, OR: Hart, pp. 37–56.

Bate, R., R. Best and A. Holmans (eds) (2000), *On the Move: The Housing Consequences of Migration*, York: Joseph Rowntree Foundation.

Belding, R.K. and D.A. Hutchison (1976), 'Home or away: why do qualified leavers from Scottish schools move away from home?', University of Kent, mimeo.

Belfield, C. and Z. Morris (1999), 'Regional migration to and from higher education institutions: scale, determinants and outcomes', *Higher Education Quarterly*, **53**(3), 240–63.

Bell, C. (1968), *Middle Class Families: Social and Geographical Mobility*, London: Routledge & Kegan Paul.

Benson, M. and K. O'Reilly (2009), 'Migration and the search for a better way of life: a critical exploration of lifestyle migration', *The Sociological Review*, **57**(4), 608–25.

Berrington, A., J. Stone and J. Falkingham (2009), 'The changing living arrangements of young adults in the UK', *Population Trends*, No. 138.

Berry, P.M., M.D.A. Rounsevell, P.A. Harrison and E. Audsley (2006), 'Assessing the vulnerability of agricultural land use and species to climate change and the role of policy in facilitating adaptation', *Environmental Science and Policy*, **9**, 189–204.

Best, R.H. and J.T. Ward (1956), *The Garden Controversy*, Wye College: Studies in Rural Land Use.

Black, R. (1998), *Refugees, Environment and Development*, London: Longmans.

Black, R. (2001), 'Environmental refugees: myth or reality?', Working Paper No. 34, UNHCR.

Black, R. et al. (2008), 'Demographics and climate change: future trends and their policy implications for migration', Brighton: University of Sussex, DRC on Migration, Globalization and Poverty, Working Paper No. T-27.

Black, R., D. Kniveton and K. Schmidt-Verkerk (2011), 'Migration and climate change: towards an integrated assessment of sensitivity', *Environment and Planning A*, **43**(2), 431–50.

Blake, S. (2009), 'Subnational patterns of population ageing', *Population Trends*, No. 136.

Boano, C., R. Zetter and T. Morris (2008), 'Environmentally displaced people: understanding the linkages between environmental change, livelihoods and forced migration', University of Oxford; Refugee Studies Centre, Forced Migration Briefing No. 1.

Boddy, M. (2007), 'Designer neighbourhoods: new build residential development in nonmetropolitan UK cities – the case of Bristol', *Environment and Planning A*, **39**(1), 86–105.

Boden, P. (1989), 'The analysis of internal migration in the United

Kingdom using Census and National Health Service Central Register data', University of Leeds, School of Geography, PhD thesis (part only).

Boden, P., J. Stillwell and P. Rees (1991), 'Internal migration projection in England: the OPCS/DOE model examined', in J. Stillwell and P. Congdon (eds), *Migration Models: Macro and Micro Approaches*, London: Belhaven, pp. 262–86.

Bogue, D.L., G. Liegel and M. Kozloski (2009), *Immigration, Internal Migration, and Local Mobility in the U.S.*, Cheltenham, UK and Northampton, MA, USA: Edward Elgar.

Boheim, R. and M.P. Taylor (2007), 'From the dark end of the street to the bright side of the road? The wage returns to migration in Britain', *Labour Economics*, **14**(1), 99–117.

Bosworth, G. (2010), 'Commercial counterurbanization: an emerging force in rural economic development', *Environment and Planning A*, **42**(4), 966–81.

Boyle, P. (1995), 'Public housing as a barrier to long-distance migration', *International Journal of Population Geography*, **1**(2), 147–64 (abstract only).

Boyle, P. (1997), 'Contrasting English and Scottish residents in the Scottish Highlands and Islands', *Scottish Geographical Magazine*, **113**(2), 98–104.

Boyle, P. (1998), 'Migration and housing tenure in South East England', *Environment and Planning A*, **30**(5), 855–66.

Boyle, P. and K. Halfacree (eds) (1998), *Migration into Rural Areas*, Chichester: Wiley.

Boyle, P., K. Halfacree and V. Robinson (1998), *Exploring Contemporary Migration*, Harlow: Addison Wesley Longman.

Bramley, G. et al. (2004), *Key Issues in Housing: Policies and Markets in the 21st Century*, Basingstoke: Palgrave.

Bramley, G., A.G. Champion and T. Fisher (2006), 'Exploring the household impacts of migration in Britain using Panel Survey data', *Regional Studies*, **40**(8), 907–26.

Bridge, G. (2010), 'Geographies of peak oil: the other carbon problem', *Geoforum*, **41**(4), 523–30.

Brown, C. and N. Glasgow (2008), *Rural Retirement Migration*, Dordrecht: Springer.

Brown, O. (2008), *Migration and Climate Change*, Geneva: IOM, Research Series No. 31.

Cairns, D. and J. Smyth (2009), 'I wouldn't mind moving actually: exploring student mobility in Northern Ireland', *International Migration*, **49**(2), 135–61.

Cameron, G. and J. Muellbauer (1998), 'The housing market and regional commuting and migration choices', *Scottish Journal of Political Economy*, **45**(4), 420–46.

Castells, M. (1993), 'European cities, the informational society, and the global economy', *Tijdschrift voor Economische en Sociale Geografie*, **84**(4), 247–57.

Castles, S. (2002), 'Environmental change and forced migration: making sense of the debate', Working Paper No. 70, Geneva: UNHCR.

Castles, S. (2010), 'Afterword: what now? Climate-induced displacement after Copenhagen', in J. McAdam (ed.), *Climate Change and Displacement: Multidisciplinary Perspectives*, Oxford and Portland, OR: Hart, pp. 239–46.

Champion, A.G. (1975), 'The United Kingdom', in R. Jones (ed.), *Essays on World Urbanization*, London: George Philip and Sons, pp. 47–66.

Champion, A.G. (1987), 'Population deconcentration in Britain 1971–84', University of Newcastle-upon-Tyne: Department of Geography Seminar Paper No. 49.

Champion, A.G. (1989a), *Counterurbanization: The Changing Pace and Nature of Population Deconcentration*, London: Edward Arnold.

Champion, A.G. (1989b), 'Internal migration and the spatial distribution of population', in H. Joshi (ed.), *The Changing Population of Britain*, Oxford: Blackwell, pp. 110–32.

Champion, A.G. (1994), 'Population change and migration in Britain since 1981: evidence for continuing deconcentration', *Environment and Planning A*, **26**(10), 1501–20 (abstract only).

Champion, A.G. (1997), 'Population deconcentration trends in Britain in the 1980s and their policy implications', in L.-E. Borgegard, A.M. Findlay and E. Sondell (eds), *Population, Planning and Policies*, Umea University: CERUM Report No. 5, pp. 31–54.

Champion, A.G. (1998), 'Studying counterurbanization and the rural population turnround', in P. Boyle and K. Halfacree (eds), *Migration into Rural Areas*, Chichester: Wiley, pp. 21–40.

Champion, A.G. (2002), 'Population change and migration in the British urban system', in H.S. Geyer (ed.), *International Handbook of Urban Systems: Studies of Urbanization and Migration in Advanced and Developing Countries*, Cheltenham, UK and Northampton, MA, USA: Edward Elgar, pp. 87–120.

Champion, A.G. (2003), 'Testing the differential urbanization model in Great Britain, 1901–91', *Tijdschrift voor Economische en Sociale Geografie*, **94**(1), 11–22.

Champion, A.G. (2004a), 'The census and the cities', *Town and Country Planning*, January, 20–22.

Champion, A.G. (2004b), 'The "counterurbanization cascade" in the UK since 1991: the evidence of a new data set', Philadelphia: AAG Annual Meeting, paper.

Champion, A.G. (2005), 'Population movement within the UK', in R. Chappell (ed.), *Focus on People and Migration*, Basingstoke: Palgrave Macmillan, pp. 92–114.

Champion, A.G. and P. Congdon (1992), 'Migration trends for the South: the emergence of a Greater South East?', in J. Stillwell, P. Rees and P. Boden (eds), *Migration Processes and Patterns: Population Redistribution in the United Kingdom*, London: Belhaven, pp. 178–204.

Champion, A.G. and M. Coombes (2010), 'Migration and socio-economic polarization within British city-regions', in J. Stillwell et al. (eds), *Technologies for Migration and Commuting Analysis*, Hershey, PA: IGI Global, pp. 196–211.

Champion, A.G. and A.J. Fielding (eds) (1992), *Migration Processes and Patterns: Research Progress and Prospects*, London: Belhaven.

Champion, A.G. and T. Fisher (2003), 'The social selectivity of migration flows affecting Britain's largest conurbations: an analysis of the 1991 Census regional migration tables', *Scottish Geographical Journal*, **119**(3), 229–46.

Champion, A.G. and A. Townsend (2011), 'The fluctuating record of economic regeneration in England's second-order city-regions, 1984–2007', *Urban Studies*, **48**(8), 1539–62.

Champion, A.G. et al. (1998), *The Determinants of Migration Flows in England: A Review of Existing Data and Evidence*, London: Department of the Environment, Transport and the Regions.

Champion, A.G. et al. (2007), *Migration and Socioeconomic Change: A 2001 Census Analysis of Britain's Larger Cities*, York: Joseph Rowntree Trust.

Champion, A.G., M. Coombes and D.L. Brown (2009), 'Migration and longer-distance commuting in rural England', *Regional Studies*, **43**(10), 1245–59.

Christian Aid (2007), *Human Tide: The Real Migration Crisis*.

Christidis, N., G.C. Donaldson and P.A. Stott (2010), 'Causes of the recent changes in cold- and heat-related mortality in England and Wales', *Climatic Change*, **102**(3–4), 539–53.

Coe, N. and A. Jones (eds) (2010), *The Economic Geography of the UK*, London: Sage.

Coleman, D. and J. Salt (1992), *The British Population: Patterns, Trends, and Processes*, Oxford: Oxford University Press.

Communion, R., A. Faggian and Q.C. Li (2010), 'Unrewarded careers in the creative class: the strange case of bohemian graduates', *Papers in Regional Science*, **89**(2), 389–410.

Compton, P. (1992), 'Migration trends for Northern Ireland: links with Great Britain', in J. Stillwell, P. Rees and P. Boden (eds), *Migration Processes and Patterns: Population Redistribution in the United Kingdom*, London: Belhaven, pp. 81–99.

Congdon, P. (1989), 'Modelling migration flows between areas: an analysis for London using the Census and OPCS Longitudinal Study', *Regional Studies*, **23**(2) 87–103.

Congdon, P. (2008), 'Models of migration age schedules: a Bayesian perspective with an application to flows between Scotland and England', in J. Raymer and F. Willekens (eds), *International Migration in Europe: Data, Models and Estimates*, Chichester: Wiley, Chapter 9.

Congdon, P. and A.G. Champion (1989), 'Trends and structure in London's migration and their relation to employment and housing markets', in P. Congdon and P. Batey (eds), *Advances in Regional Demography: Information, Forecasts, Models*, London: Belhaven, pp. 180–204.

Conway, G., J. Waage and S. Delaney (2010), 'Adapting to climate change', *Science and Innovation for Development*, London: UKCDS, pp. 301–54.

Conway, J. and E. Ramsay (1986), *A Job to Move: The Housing Problems of Job Seekers*, London: SHAC.

Cooke, T.J. (2011), 'It is not just the economy: declining migration and the rise of secular rootedness', *Population, Space and Place*, **17**(3), 193–203.

Coombes, M. and M. Charlton (1992), 'Flows to and from London: a decade of change?', in J. Stillwell, P. Rees and P. Boden (eds), *Migration Processes and Patterns: Population Redistribution in the United Kingdom*, London: Belhaven, pp. 56–80.

Daoust, P. (2010), 'The rise of home working', *The Guardian*, 3 August 2010.

Day, G., H. Davis and A. Drakakis-Smith (2010), '"There's one shop you don't go into if you are English": the social and political integration of English migrants into Wales', *Journal of Ethnic and Migration Studies*, **36**(9), 1405–23.

Dennett, A. (2010), 'Understanding internal migration in Britain at the start of the 21st century', University of Leeds, PhD thesis.

Dennett, A. (2011), 'Understanding a decade of internal migration in Britain at the start of the 21st century – from spatial interaction to life course explanations', 6th International Population Geographies Conference, Umea, Sweden.

Dennett, A. and P. Rees (2010), 'Estimates of internal migration flows for the UK, 2000–2007', *Population Trends*, No. 140, 82–105.

Dennett, A. and J. Stillwell (2008), 'Population turnover and churn:

enhancing understanding of internal migration in Britain through measures of stability', *Population Trends*, No. 134.

Dennett, A. and J. Stillwell (2010), 'Internal migration patterns by age and sex at the start of the 21st century', in J. Stillwell, O. Duke-Williams and A. Dennett (eds), *Technologies for Migration and Commuting Analysis: Spatial Interaction Data Applications*, Hershey, PA: IGI Global, pp. 153–74.

Dennett, A. and J. Stillwell (2011), 'Internal migration in Britain, 2000–01, examined through an area classification framework', *Population, Space and Place*, **16**(6), 517–38.

Deschenes, O. and E. Moretti (2009), 'Extreme weather events, mortality, and migration', *Review of Economics and Statistics*, **91**(4), 659–81.

Donovan, N., T. Pilch and T. Rubenstein (2002), 'Geographic mobility', Mobility Paper, UK Cabinet Office: Performance and Innovation Unit.

Dorling, D. and B. Thomas (2011), *Bankrupt Britain: An Atlas of Social Change*, Bristol: Polity Press.

Dow, K. and T.E. Downing (2007), *The Atlas of Climate Change*, London: Earthscan.

Dowling, F. (2007), 'The economics of climate change', lecture given to the Chevening Fellows at the University of Reading, 21 February 2007 (PowerPoint presentation).

Duke-Williams, O. (2009), 'The geographies of student migration in the UK', *Environment and Planning A*, **41**(8), 1826–48.

Duncan, S. and M. Phillips (2010), 'People who live apart together (LATs), how different are they?', *Sociological Review*, **58**(1), 112–34.

Duncan, S. and D. Smith (2002), 'Geographies of family formations: spatial differences and gender cultures in Britain', *Transactions of the Institute of British Geographers*, **27**(4), 471–93.

Dunford, M. and Fielding, A.J. (1997), 'Greater London, the Southeast region and the wider Britain: metropolitan polarization, uneven development and inter-regional migration', in H.H. Blotevogel and A.J. Fielding (eds), *People, Jobs and Mobility in the New Europe*, Chichester: Wiley, pp. 247–76.

Environment Agency (2009), 'Thames Estuary 2100: managing flood risk through London and the Thames Estuary', available at: http://www.environment-agency.gov.uk/homeandleisure/floods/104695.aspx; accessed 4 January 2012.

Erturk, I., J. Froud, S. Johal, A. Leaver, M. Moran and K. Williams (2011), 'City state against national settlement: UK economic policy and politics after the financial crisis', Open University CRESC Working Paper Series No. 101.

ESRC Seminar Series (2009), 'How will climate change affect people in the UK and how can we best develop an equitable response?', 30 November, London.

European Union (EU) (2008), 'Preliminary findings from the EACH-FOR project on environmentally induced migration'.

Evandrou, M., J. Falkingham and M. Green (2010), 'Migration in later life: evidence from the British Household Panel Study', *Population Trends*, No. 141, 77–94.

Faggian, A. and P. McCann (2006), 'Human capital flows and regional knowledge assets: a simultaneous equations approach', *Oxford Economic Papers*, **58**(3), 475–500.

Faggian, A. and P. McCann (2009a), 'Human capital, graduate migration and innovation in British regions', *Cambridge Journal of Economics*, **33**(2), 317–33.

Faggian, A. and P. McCann (2009b), 'Universities, agglomerations and graduate human capital mobility', *Tijdschrift voor Economische en Sociale Geographie*, **100**(2), 210–23.

Faggian, A., P. McCann and S. Sheppard (2007), 'Some evidence that women are more mobile than men: gender differences in UK graduate migration behaviour', *Journal of Regional Science*, **47**(3), 517–39.

Feldman, M.P. (2002), 'The internet revolution and the geography of innovation', *International Social Science Journal*, **54**(171), 47–56.

Feng, S., A.B. Krueger and M. Oppenheimer (2010), 'Linkages among climate change, crop yields and Mexico–US cross-border migration', *Proceedings of the National Academy of Sciences*, **107**(32), 14257–62.

Fielding, A.J. (1966), 'Internal migration and regional economic growth: a case study of France', *Urban Studies*, **3**(1), 200–214.

Fielding, A.J. (1971), 'Internal migration in England and Wales', London: Centre for Environmental Studies, CES UWP No. 14, 92.

Fielding, A.J. (1975), 'Internal migration in Western Europe', in L.A. Kosinski and R.M. Prothero (eds), *People on the Move: Studies on Internal Migration*, London: Methuen, pp. 237–54.

Fielding, A.J. (1982), *Counterurbanization in Western Europe, Progress in Planning*, Vol. 17, Oxford: Pergamon Press.

Fielding, A.J. (1989), 'Population redistribution in Western Europe: trends since 1950 and the debate about counterurbanization', in P. Congdon and P. Batey (eds), *Advances in Regional Demography: Information, Forecasts, Models*, London: Belhaven, pp. 167–79.

Fielding, A.J. (1992a), 'Migration and social change', in J. Stillwell, P. Rees and P. Boden (eds), *Migration Processes and Patterns: Population Redistribution in the United Kingdom*, London: Belhaven, pp. 225–47.

Fielding, A.J. (1992b), 'Migration and social mobility: South East England as an escalator region', *Regional Studies*, **26**(1), 1–15.

Fielding, A.J. (1992c), 'Migration and culture', in A.G. Champion and A.J. Fielding (eds), *Migration Processes and Patterns*, Vol. 1, London: Belhaven Press, pp. 201–14.

Fielding, A.J. (1993), 'Migration and the metropolis: an empirical and theoretical analysis of migration to and from South East England', *Progress in Planning*, **39**(2), 71–166.

Fielding A.J. (1995), 'Migration and middle class formation in England and Wales, 1981–91', in T. Butler and M. Savage (eds), *Social Change and the Middle Classes*, London: UCL Press, pp. 169–87.

Fielding, A.J. (1997), 'The effects of economic restructuring on the populations of Western Europe's cities and regions', in II.II. Blotevogel and A.J. Fielding (eds), *People, Jobs and Mobility in the New Europe*, Chichester: Wiley, pp. 297–304.

Fielding, A.J. (1998a), 'Counterurbanization and social class', in P. Boyle and K. Halfacree (eds), *Migration into Rural Areas*, Chichester: Wiley, pp. 41–60.

Fielding, A.J. (1998b), 'Gender, class and region in England and Wales: a longitudinal analysis', *Ritsumeikan Chirigaku*, **10**, 1–22.

Fielding, A.J. (2007), 'Migration and social mobility in urban systems: national and international trends', in H.S. Geyer (ed.), *International Handbook of Urban Policy*, Cheltenham, UK and Northampton, MA, USA: Edward Elgar, pp. 107–37.

Fielding, A.J. (2010), 'Migration at a time of crisis: a simple conceptual model applied to East Asian migrations', paper presented at the Royal Geographical Society Annual Conference, London.

Fielding, A.J. and S. Halford (1993), 'Geographies of opportunity: a regional analysis of gender-specific social and spatial mobilities in England and Wales, 1971–81', *Environment and Planning A*, **25**(10), 1421–40.

Fielding, A.J. and Y. Ishikawa (2003), 'Migration and the life course in contemporary Japan', *Geographical Review of Japan*, **76**(12), 882–93.

Findlay, A. and R. Rogerson (1993), 'Migration, places and quality of life', in A.G. Champion (ed.), *Population Matters*, London: Paul Chapman, pp. 33–49.

Findlay, A. et al. (2001), 'Mobility as a driver of change in rural Britain: an analysis of the links between migration, commuting and travel to shop patterns', *International Journal of Population Geography*, **7**(1), 1–16.

Findlay, A., A. Stockdale and E. Stewart (2002), 'Professional and managerial migration from core to periphery: the case of English migration to Scottish cities', *International Journal of Population Geography*, **8**(3), 217–32.

Findlay, A. et al. (2008), 'Getting off the escalator? A study of Scots out-migration from a global city region', *Environment and Planning A*, **40**(9), 2169–85.

Finney, N. and L. Simpson (2008), 'Internal migration and ethnic groups: evidence for Britain from the 2001 Census', *Population, Space and Place*, **14**(2), 63–83.

Finney, N. and L. Simpson (2009), *Sleepwalking to Segregation? Challenging Myths about Race and Migration*, Bristol: Policy Press.

Flowerdew, R. (1992), 'Labour market operation and geographical mobility', in A.G. Champion and A.J. Fielding (eds), *Migration Processes and Patterns: Research Prospects and Progress*, London: Belhaven Press, pp. 135–47.

Flowerdew, R. and P. Boyle (1992), 'Migration trends for the West Midlands: suburbanization, counterurbanization or rural depopulation?', in J. Stillwell, P. Rees and P. Boden (eds), *Migration Processes and Patterns: Population Redistribution in the United Kingdom*, London: Belhaven, pp. 144–61.

Forrest, R. (1987), 'Spatial mobility, tenure mobility, and emerging social divisions in the UK housing market', *Environment and Planning A*, **19**(12), 1611–30.

Forrest, R. and A. Murie (1992), 'Housing as a barrier to the geographical mobility of labour', in A.G. Champion and A.J. Fielding (eds), *Migration Processes and Patterns: Research Prospects and Progress*, London: Belhaven Press, pp. 77–103.

Forrest, R. et al. (1991), 'Labour mobility and housing provision: a review of the literature', University of Bristol: School for Advanced Urban Studies, Working Paper No. 98.

Fotheringham, S. (1991), 'Migration and spatial structure: the development of the competing destinations model', in J. Stillwell and P. Congdon (eds), *Migration Models*, London: Belhaven Press, pp. 57–72.

Frazier et al. (2010), 'Influence of potential sea level rise on social vulnerability to hurricane storm-surge hazards, Sarasota County, Florida', *Applied Geography*, **30**(4), 490–505.

Fritz, C. (2010), 'Climate change and migration: sorting through complex issues without the hype', Washington DC: Migration Policy Institute.

Fruhmann, J. and J. Jager (2010), 'Linking the earth's future to migration: scenarios of environmental change and possible impacts on forced migration', in T. Afifi and J. Jager (eds), *Environment, Forced Migration and Social Vulnerability*, Berlin/Heidelberg: Springer-Verlag, pp. 247–62.

Gemenne, F. (2009), *Geopolitique du Changement Climatique*, Paris: Armand Colin.

Gemenne, F. (2010), 'What's in a name: social vulnerabilities and refugee controversy in the wake of Hurricane Katrina', in T. Afifi and J. Jager (eds), *Environment, Forced Migration and Social Vulnerability*, Berlin/ Heidelberg: Springer-Verlag, pp. 29–40.

Gething, P.W. et al. (2010), 'Climate change and the global malaria recession', *Nature*, **465**(7296), 342–5.

Geyer, H.S. (2002), 'An exploration in migration theory', in H.S. Geyer (ed.), *International Handbook of Urban Systems: Studies of Urbanization and Migration in Advanced and Developing Countries*, Cheltenham, UK and Northampton, MA, USA: Edward Elgar, pp. 19–38.

Glaser, K. and E. Grundy (1998), 'Migration and household change in the population aged 65 and over, 1971–91', *International Journal of Population Geography*, **4**(4), 323–39.

Glynn, A. (2007), 'Explaining labor's declining share of national income', *G-24 Policy Brief*, No. 4.

Gordon, I. (1982), 'The analysis of motivation-specific migration streams', *Environment and Planning A*, **14**(1), 5–20 (abstract only).

Gordon, I. (1990), 'Housing and labour market constraints on migration across the north/south divide', in J. Ermisch (ed.), *Housing and the National Economy*, London: NIESR, pp. 75–89.

Gordon, I. (1992), 'Modelling approaches to migration and the labour market', in A.G. Champion and A.J. Fielding (eds), *Migration Processes and Patterns: Research Progress and Prospects*, London: Belhaven, pp. 119–34.

Graham, E. and P. Boyle (2003), 'Scotland's demographic regime: population and the politics of devolution', *Scottish Geographical Journal*, **119**(4), 361–82.

Green, A. (1992a), 'Changing labour processes and migration', in A.G. Champion and A.J. Fielding (eds), *Migration Processes and Patterns: Research Prospects and Progress*, London: Belhaven Press, pp. 105–18.

Green, A. (1992b), 'Migration trends for Wales: rural revival?', in J. Stillwell, P. Rees and P. Boden (eds), *Migration Processes and Patterns: Population Redistribution in the United Kingdom*, London: Belhaven, pp. 129–43.

Green, A. (1995), 'The geography of dual-career households: a research agenda and selected evidence from secondary data sources for Britain', *International Journal of Population Geography*, **1**(1), 29–50.

Green, A. (1997), 'A question of compromise? Case study evidence on the location and mobility strategies of dual career households', *Regional Studies*, **31**(7), 641–57.

Green, A. (1999a), 'Employment opportunities and constraints facing in-migrants to rural areas in England', *Geography*, **84**(1), 34–44.

Green, A. (1999b), 'Longer-distance commuting as a substitute for migration in Britain: a review of trends, issues and implications', *International Journal of Population Geography*, **5**(1) 49–67.

Green, A. (2004), 'Is relocation redundant? Observations on the changing nature and impacts of employment-related geographical mobility in the UK', *Regional Studies*, **38**(6), 629–41.

Green, A. (2006), 'Employment and the older person in the countryside', in P. Lowe and L. Speakman (eds), *The Ageing Countryside: The Growing Older Population of Rural England*, London: Age Concern, pp. 94–118.

Green, A. and A. Canny (2003), *Geographical Mobility: Family Impacts*, York: Joseph Rowntree Foundation.

Green, A., T. Hogarth and R. Shackleton (1999), *Long Distance Living: Dual Location Households*, Bristol: Policy Press.

Green, A. et al. (2009), 'Rural development and labour supply challenges in the UK: the role of non-UK migrants', *Regional Studies*, **43**(10), 1261–73.

Green, T. and A. Winters (2010), 'Economic crises and migration: learning from the past and the present', *The World Economy*, **33**(9), 1053–72.

Grimsrud, G.M. (2011), 'Gendered spaces on trial: the influence of regional gender contracts on in-migration of women to rural Norway', *Geografiska Annaler B*, **93**(1), 3–20.

Grundy, E. (1987), 'Retirement migration and its consequences in England and Wales', *Ageing and Society*, **7**(1), 57–82 (abstract only).

Grundy, E. (1992), 'The household dimension in migration research', in A.G. Champion and A.J. Fielding (eds), *Migration Processes and Patterns: Research Prospects and Progress*, London: Belhaven Press, pp. 165–74.

Gutmann, M.P. and Field, V. (2010), 'Katrina in historical context: environment and migration in the US', *Population and Environment*, **31**(1–3), 3–19.

Haines, A., R.S. Kovats, D. Campbell-Lendrum and C. Corvalan (2006), 'Climate change and human health: impacts, vulnerability and mitigation', *The Lancet*, **367**(9528), 2101–9.

Hakim, C. (2010), 'Erotic capital', *European Sociological Review*, **26**(5), 499–518.

Halfacree, K. (2008), 'To revitalize counterurbanization research? Recognizing an international and fuller picture', *Population, Space and Place*, **14**, 479–95.

Hallegatte, S. et al. (2008), 'Assessing climate change impacts, sea level rise and storm surge risk in port cities: a study of Copenhagen', OECD: Environment Working Papers No. 3.

Halliday, J. and M. Coombes (1995), 'In search of counterurbanization:

some evidence from Devon on the relationship between patterns of migration and motivation', *Journal of Rural Studies*, **11**(4), 433–46.

Hamnett, P. (1992), 'House-price differentials, housing wealth and migration', in A.G. Champion and A.J. Fielding (eds), *Migration Processes and Patterns: Research Prospects and Progress*, London: Belhaven Press, pp. 55–64.

Hardill, I. (2002), 'Moving experiences: intensified mobility and dual-career households', St Andrews University: Population Geography Conference, July.

Hartmann, B. (2010), 'Rethinking climate refugees and climate conflict: rhetoric, reality and the politics of policy discourse', *Journal of International Development*, **22**(2), 233–46.

Harvey, L.D.D. (2010), 'An overview of climate change science in 1977 marking the publication of Volume 100 of Climatic Change', *Climatic Change*, **100**(1), 15–21.

Hatton, T.J. and Tani, M. (2005), 'Immigration and inter-regional mobility in the UK 1982–2000', *The Economic Journal*, **115**(507), 342–58.

Hayes, L., A. Al-Hamad and A. Geddes (1995), 'Marriage, divorce and residential change: evidence from the household sample of anonymised records', Brighton: British Society for Population Studies Conference.

Henry, S., P. Boyle and E.F. Lambin (2003), 'Modelling inter-provincial migration in Burkina Faso: the role of socio-demographic and environmental factors', *Applied Geography*, **23**(3), 115–36.

Hickingbotham, A. and A. Strachan (1991), 'Charting counterurbanization: the case of Powys', Midlands Regional Research Laboratory.

Higher Education Funding Council for England (HEFCE) (2010), *Regional Profiles of Higher Education 2007–08*, London: HEFCE.

Hoare, A.G. (1991), 'University competition, student migration and regional economic differentials in the United Kingdom', *Higher Education*, **22**(4), 351–70.

Hoare, A.G. (1994), 'Transferred skills and university excellence: an exploratory analysis of the geography of mobility of UK academic staff', *Geografiska Annaler*, **76**(3), 143–60.

Hoare, A. and M. Corver (2010), 'The regional geography of new young graduate labour in the UK', *Regional Studies*, **44**(4), 477–94.

Hoggart, K. (1997), 'The middle classes in rural England, 1971–91', *Journal of Rural Studies*, **13**(3), 253–73.

Hoggart, K. (2007), 'The diluted working classes of rural England and Wales', *Journal of Rural Studies*, **23**(3), 305–17.

Hollywood, E. et al. (2007), 'Demographic and labour market change: the dynamics of older workers in the Scottish labour market', *Scottish Geographical Journal*, **123**(4), 242–56.

Holman, I.P. et al. (2005), 'A regional, multi-sectoral and integrated assessment of the impacts of climate and socio-economic change in the UK (Part II: Results)', *Climatic Change*, **71**(1), 43–73.

Hughes, G. and B. McCormick (1981), 'Do council house policies reduce migration between regions', *Economic Journal*, **91**(364), 919–39.

Hughes, G. and B. McCormick (1987), 'Housing markets, unemployment and labour market flexibility in the UK', *European Economic Review*, **31**(3), 615–45.

Hughes, G. and B. McCormick (1990), 'Housing and labour market mobility', in J. Ermisch (ed.), *Housing and the National Economy*, Aldershot: Avebury, pp. 94–112.

Hugo, G. (1996), 'Environmental concerns and international migration', *International Migration Review*, **30**(1), 105–31.

Hugo, G. (2008), 'Migration, development and environment', at the PERN Cyberseminar 'Environmentally induced population displacements', 18–29 August 2008, available at: http://www.populationenvir onmentresearch.org; accessed 4 January 2012.

Hussain, S. and J. Stillwell (2008), 'Internal migration of ethnic groups in England and Wales by age and district type', University of Leeds, School of Geography, Working Paper No. 08/03.

Intergovernmental Panel on Climate Change (IPCC) (2000), *IPCC Special Report: Emissions Scenarios. Summary for Policymakers*, WMO/UNEP.

Intergovernmental Panel on Climate Change (IPCC) (2001), *Climate Change 2001: Impacts, Adaptation and Vulnerability*, Geneva: World Meteorological Organization (IPCC).

Intergovernmental Panel on Climate Change (IPCC) (2007), 'Summary for policy makers', in S. Solomon et al. (eds), *Climate Change 2007: The Physical Science Basis*, Cambridge: Cambridge University Press.

International Labour Office (2010), *Global Wage Report 2010/2011*, Geneva: ILO.

International Organization for Migration (2009), *Migration, Environment and Climate Change: Assessing the Evidence*, Geneva: IOM.

Jackman, R. and S. Savouri (1992), 'Regional migration in Britain: an analysis of gross flows using NHS Central Register data', *Economic Journal*, **102**(415), 1433–50.

Jasparro, C. and J. Taylor (2008), 'Climate change and regional vulnerability to transnational security threats in Southeast Asia', *Geopolitics*, **15**(3), 232–56.

Jenkins, J. (1992), 'Migration trends for the East Midlands: the dynamics of a growth region', in J. Stillwell, P. Rees and P. Boden (eds), *Migration Processes and Patterns: Population Redistribution in the United Kingdom*, London: Belhaven, pp. 162–77.

Jennings, T.L. (2009), 'Exploring the invisibility of local knowledge in decision-making: the Boscastle Harbour flood disaster', in W.N. Adger, I. Lorenzoni and K.L. O'Brien (eds), *Adapting to Climate Change: Thresholds, Values, Governance*, Cambridge: Cambridge University Press, pp. 240–54.

Jivraj, S. and N. Marquis (2009), 'A comparison of internal migration data derived from the Pupil Level Annual School Census with the National Health Service Central Register and 2001 Census data', University of Manchester: Centre for Census and Survey Research, Working Paper No. 2009-04.

Johnson, J.H. and J. Salt (1980a), 'Labour migration within organizations: an introductory study', *Tijdschrift voor Economische en Sociale Geografie*, **71**(5), 277–84.

Johnson, J.H. and J. Salt (1980b), 'Employment transfer policies in Great Britain', *Three Banks Review*, 18–39.

Johnston, R.J. (1989), 'The southward drift: preliminary analyses of the career patterns of 1980 graduates in Great Britain', *Geography*, **74**(3), 239–44.

Jones, C. and B. Armitage (1990), 'Population change within area types: England and Wales 1971–81', *Population Trends*, No. 60, 25–32.

Jones, G. (2001), 'Migration or staying on? Decision-making and behaviour of young people in rural Scotland', *Sociology*, **33**(1), 1–22.

Jones, H. (1992), 'Migration trends for Scotland: central losses and peripheral gains', in J. Stillwell, P. Rees and P. Boden (eds), *Migration Processes and Patterns: Population Redistribution in the United Kingdom*, London: Belhaven, pp. 100–14.

Jones, H. et al. (1986), 'Peripheral counterurbanization: findings from an integration of census and survey data in northern Scotland', *Regional Studies*, **20**(1), 15–26.

Jones, P.S. and A.E. Green (200), 'The quantity and quality of jobs: changes in UK regions, 1997–2007', *Environment and Planning A*, **41**(10), 2474–95.

Kalin, W. (2010), 'Conceptualizing climate-induced displacement', in J. McAdam (ed.), *Climate Change and Displacement: Multidisciplinary Perspectives*, Oxford and Portland, OR: Hart, pp. 81–104.

Karl, T.R., J.M. Melilo and T.C. Peterson (eds) (2009), *Global Climate Change Impacts in the United States*, New York: Cambridge University Press.

King, R., R. Black, M. Collyer, A.J. Fielding and R. Skeldon (2010), *People on the Move: An Atlas of Migration*, Berkeley: University of California Press.

Kintrea, K. (2005), 'Visions of housing futures: incipient obsolescence?', University of York, Housing Studies Association Conference.

Kitching, R. (1990), 'Migration behaviour among the unemployed and low-skilled', in J.H. Johnson and J. Salt (eds), *Labour Migration*, London: David Fulton, pp. 172–90.

Kniveton, D. et al. (2008), *Climate Change and Migration: Improving Methodologies to Estimate Flows*, Geneva: IOM, Research Series No. 33.

Kono, S. and M. Shio (1965), *Inter-Prefectural Migration in Japan: Migration Stream Analysis*, Bombay: Demographic Training and Research Centre/London: Asia Publishing House.

Kowalczuk, K. (2010), 'Population growth in a high amenity area: migration and socio-economic change in Cornwall', University of Plymouth: School of Applied Psychosocial Sciences PhD.

Laczko, F. and C. Aghazarm (2010), *Migration, Environment and Climate Change: Assessing the Evidence*, Geneva: IOM.

Lancet/UCL (2009), 'Managing the health effects of climate change', *The Lancet*, **373**(9676), 1693–733.

Laurian, L. (2008), 'The distribution of environmental risks: analytical methods and French data', *Population* (English Edition), **63**(4), 617–34.

Lee, E. (1969), 'A theory of migration', in J.A. Jackson (ed.), *Migration*, Cambridge: Cambridge University Press, pp. 282–97.

Lewis, G.I. (2000), 'Changing places in a rural world: the population turnround in perspective', *Geography*, **85**(2), 157–65.

Lin, C.-Y.C. (2010), 'Instability, investment, disasters and demography: natural disasters and fertility in Italy (1820–1962) and Japan (1671–1965)', *Population and Environment*, **31**(4), 255–81.

Lind, H. (1969), 'Internal migration in Britain', in J.A. Jackson (ed.), *Migration*, Cambridge: Cambridge University Press, pp. 74–98.

Lu, X., J. Crossley and M. Hulme (2001), 'An exploration of regional climate change scenarios for Scotland', *Scottish Geographical Journal*, **117**(4), 251–70.

Lundholm, E. (2007), 'Are movers still the same? Characteristics of inter-regional migrants in Sweden 1970–2001', *Tijdschrift voor Economische en Sociale Geografie*, **98**(3), 336–48.

Marchiori, L. and I. Schumacher (2009), 'When nature rebels: international migration, climate change and inequality', Paris: Ecole Polytechnique: Département d'Economie, Paper No. 2009-04.

Martin, S.F. (2010), 'Climate change and international migration', Washington DC: The German Marshall Fund of the United States, Study Team on Climate-induced Migration.

Masser, I. (1970), 'A test of some models for predicting intermetropolitan movement of population in England and Wales', London: Centre for Environmental Studies, University Working Paper No. 9.

Massey, D. (2007), *World City*, Cambridge: Polity Press.

Massey, D., W.G. Axinn and D.J. Ghimire (2010), 'Environmental change and out-migration: evidence from Nepal', *Population and Environment*, **32**(2–3), 109–36.

Matheson, J. (2009), 'National Statistician's annual article on the population: a demographic review', *Population Trends*, No. 138, 7–22.

McAdam, J. (ed.) (2010), *Climate Change and Displacement: Multidisciplinary Perspectives*, Oxford and Portland, OR: Hart.

McGranahan, G., D. Balk and B. Anderson (2007), 'The rising tide: assessing the risks of climate change and human settlements in low elevation coastal zones', *Environment and Urbanization*, **19**(1), 17–37.

McLeman, R. (2009), 'Climate change and adaptive human migration: lessons from rural North America', in W.N. Adger, I. Lorenzoni and K.L. O'Brien (eds), *Adapting to Climate Change: Thresholds, Values, Governance*, Cambridge: Cambridge University Press, pp. 296–310.

McLeman, R. (2010), 'Impacts of population change on vulnerability and the capacity to adapt to climate change and variability: a typology based on lessons from "a hard country"', *Population and Environment*, **31**(5), 286–316.

McLeman, R. and B. Smit (2006), 'Migration as an adaptation to climate change', *Climate Change*, **76**(1–2), 31–53.

McMichael, A.J. et al. (2010), 'Climate-related displacement: health risks and responses', in J. McAdam (ed.), *Climate Change and Displacement: Multidisciplinary Perspectives*, Oxford and Portland, OR: Hart, pp. 191–220.

Mearns, R. and A. Norton (eds) (2010), *Social Dimensions of Climate Change*, Washington DC: World Bank.

Meen, G. (1999), 'Regional house prices and the ripple effect: a new interpretation', *Housing Studies*, **14**(6), 733–53.

Mesnard, A. and P. Seabright (2009), 'Escaping epidemics through migration? Quarantine measures under incomplete information and infection risk', *Journal of Public Economics*, **93**(7–8), 931–8.

Milbourne, P. (2007), 'Re-populating rural studies: migrations, movements and mobilities', *Journal of Rural Studies*, **23**(3), 381–6.

Millington, J. (2000), 'Migration and age: the effect of age on sensitivity to migration stimuli', *Regional Studies*, **34**(6), 521–33.

Mitchell, C. (2004), 'Making sense of counterurbanization', *Journal of Rural Studies*, **20**(1), 15–34.

Molho, I. and I. Gordon (1987), 'The changing pattern of inter-regional migration in Great Britain, 1960–86', mimeo.

Morrissey, J. (2009), 'Environmental change and forced migration: a state of the art review', Oxford University: Refugee Studies Centre.

Mosca, I. and R.E. Wright (2010), 'National and international graduate migration flows', *Population*, **141**(1), 36–52.

Moser, S.C. (2010), 'Now more than ever: the need for more societally relevant research on vulnerability and adaptation to climate change', *Applied Geography*, **30**(4), 464–74.

Muellbauer, J. and A. Murphy (1988), 'UK house prices and migration: economics and investment implications', research paper, Oxford: Nuffield College.

Munro, M. (1992), 'Housing market restructuring: consequences for migration', in A.G. Champion and A.J. Fielding (eds), *Migration Processes and Patterns: Research Prospects and Progress*, London: Belhaven Press, pp. 41–54.

Munro, M., I. Turok and M. Livingston (2009), 'Students in cities: a preliminary analysis of their patterns and effects', *Environment and Planning A*, **41**(8), 1805–25.

Murdoch, J. and G. Day (1998), 'Middle class mobility, rural communities and the politics of exclusion', in P. Boyle and K. Halfacree (eds), *Migration into Rural Areas*, Chichester: Wiley, pp. 186–99.

Myers, N. (1997), 'Environmental refugees', *Population and Environment*, **19**(2), 167–82.

Nicholls, R.J. (2003), 'Case study on sea-level rise impacts', OECD: Working Party on Global and Structural Policies.

Nicholls, R.J. et al. (2008), 'Ranking port cities with high exposure and vulnerability to climate extremes: exposure estimates', OECD: Environment Working Papers No. 1.

Nicholson-Cole, S. and T. O'Riordon (2009), 'Adaptive governance for a changing coastline: science, policy and publics in search of a sustainable future', in W.N. Adger, I. Lorenzoni and K.L. O'Brien (eds), *Adapting to Climate Change: Thresholds, Values, Governance*, Cambridge: Cambridge University Press, pp. 368–83.

Northern Ireland Statistics and Research Agency (NISRA) (2010), *Population and Migration Estimates Northern Ireland 2009 – Statistical Report*, Belfast: NISRA.

Nygaard, C. (2011), 'International migration, housing demand and access to home ownership in the UK', *Urban Studies*, **48**(11), 2211–29.

O'Brien et al. (2008), *Disaster Risk Reduction, Climate Change Adaptation and Human Security*, University of Oslo: Report No. 2008:3.

Office of Population Censuses and Surveys (OPCS) (1983), *Recently Moving Households: A Follow-up to the 1978 National Dwelling and Household Survey*, London: HMSO.

Owen, D. (1992), 'Migration and employment', in J. Stillwell, P. Rees and P. Boden (eds), *Migration Processes and Patterns: Population Redistribution in the United Kingdom*, London: Belhaven, pp. 205–24.

Owen, D. and A. Green (1992), 'Migration patterns and trends', in A.G. Champion and A.J. Fielding (eds), *Migration Processes and Patterns: Research Prospects and Progress*, London: Belhaven Press, pp. 17–38.

Pellegrini, P.A. and A.S. Fotheringham (2002), 'Modelling spatial choice: a review and synthesis in a migration context', *Progress in Human Geography*, **26**(4), 487–510.

Perch-Nielsen, S. (2004), 'Understanding the effect of climate change on human migration: the contribution of mathematical and conceptual models', Diploma thesis, Swiss Federal Institute of Technology, Zurich.

Perch-Nielsen, S., M. Battig and D. Imboden (2008), 'Exploring the link between climate change and migration', *Climatic Change*, **91**(3–4), 375–93.

Phillips, M. (2002), 'The production, symbolization and socialization of gentrification: impressions from two Berkshire villages', *Transactions of the Institute of British Geographers*, **27**(3), 282–308.

Phillips, M. (2005), 'Differential productions of rural gentrification: illustrations from North and South Norfolk', *Geoforum*, **36**(4), 477–94.

Phillips, M. (2007), 'Changing class complexions on and in the British countryside', *Journal of Rural Studies*, **23**(3), 283–304.

Piguet, E. (2008), 'Climate change and forced migration: new issues in refugee research', Geneva: UNHCR Research Paper No. 153.

Piguet, E. (2010a), 'Linking climate change, environmental degradation, and migration: a methodological overview', available at: wires.wiley.com/climatechange; accessed 4 January 2012.

Piguet, E. (2010b), 'Climate and migration: a synthesis', in T. Afifi and J. Jager (eds), *Environment, Forced Migration and Social Vulnerability*, Berlin/Heidelberg: Springer-Verlag, pp. 73–85.

Piguet, E. and A. Picoud (2011), *Migration and Climate Change*, Cambridge: Cambridge University Press.

Pissarides, C. and J. Wadsworth (1989), 'Unemployment and the inter-regional mobility of labour', *Economic Journal*, **99**(397), 739–55.

Pittock, A.B. (2009), *Climate Change: The Science, Impacts and Solutions*, London: Earthscan (second edition).

Plane, D.A. and P.A. Rogerson (1994), *The Geographical Analysis of Population*, New York: Wiley.

Rabe, B. and M. Taylor (2010), 'Differences in opportunities? Wage, unemployment and house-price effects on migration', University of Essex: Institute for Social and Economic Research, Working Paper No. 2010-05.

Raleigh, C. and L. Jordan (2010), 'Climate change and migration: emerging patterns in the developing world', in R. Mearns and A. Norton (eds), *Social Dimensions of Climate Change*, Washington DC: World Bank, pp. 103–32.

Raleigh, C., L. Jordan and I. Salehyan (2008), 'Assessing the impact of climate change on migration and conflict', paper presented at 'Social Dimensions of Climate Change' conference, Washington DC: World Bank.

Ravenstein, E.G. (1885), 'The laws of migration', *Journal of the Statistical Society*, **158**(2), 167–235.

Raymer, J. and C. Giulietti (2010), 'Analysing structures of interregional migration in England', in J. Stillwell et al. (eds), *Technologies for Migration and Commuting Analysis*, Hershey, PA: IGI Global, pp. 80–293.

Raymer, J., P.W.F. Smith and C. Giulietti (2011), 'Combining census and registration data to analyse ethnic migration patterns in England from 1991 to 2007', *Population, Space and Place*, **17**(1), 73–88.

Reeder, T. et al. (2009), 'Protecting London from tidal flooding: limits to engineering adaptation', in W.N. Adger, I. Lorenzoni and K.L. O'Brien (eds), *Adapting to Climate Change: Thresholds, Values, Governance*, Cambridge: Cambridge University Press, pp. 54–63.

Rees, P. (1992), 'Elderly migration and population redistribution in the United Kingdom', in A. Rogers (ed.), *Elderly Migration and Population Redistribution*, London: Belhaven Press, pp. 203–25.

Rees, P. (2008), 'What happens when international migrants settle? Projections of ethnic groups in United Kingdom regions', in J. Raymer and F. Willekens (eds), *International Migration in Europe*, Chichester: John Wiley, pp. 329–69.

Rees, P. and D. Phillips (1996), 'Geographical spread, spatial concentration and internal migration', in P. Ratcliffe (ed.), *Ethnicity in the 1991 Census: Social Geography and Ethnicity in Britain*, London: Stationery Office (ONS), pp. 23–109.

Rees, P., J. Stillwell and P. Boden (1989), 'Migration trends and population projections for the elderly', in P. Congdon and P. Batey (eds), *Advances in Regional Demography: Information, Forecasts, Models*, London: Belhaven, pp. 205–28.

Rees, P., J. Stillwell and P. Boden (1992), 'Migration trends for the North: patterns identified and processes distinguished', in J. Stillwell, P. Rees and P. Boden (eds), *Migration Processes and Patterns: Population Redistribution in the United Kingdom*, London: Belhaven, pp. 115–28.

Rees, P., D. Vickers and J. Jin (2006), 'Trends in migration to and from Scotland: an analysis', University of Liverpool: Third International Population Geography Conference.

Rees, P., P. Wohland and P. Boden (2010), *Report on Climate Change and Migration Scenario*, ESPON 2013 Programme, DEMIFER, ARP 2013/1/3.

Reid, A. and C. Miller (2010/11), 'Regional characteristics of foreign-born people living in the United Kingdom', *Regional Trends*, No. 43, 1–30.

Renaud, F., J.J. Bogardi, O. Dun and K. Warner (2007), 'Control, adapt or flee: how to face environmental migration', Bonn: United Nations University, Institute for Environment and Human Security, Intersections No. 5/2007.

Reuveny, R. (2007), 'Climate change-induced migration and violent conflict', *Political Geography*, **26**(6), 656–73.

Reuveny, R. and W.H. Moore (2009), 'Does environmental degradation influence migration? Emigration to developed countries in the late 1980s and 1990s', *Social Science Quarterly*, **90**(3), 461–79.

Risk Management Solutions (RMS) (2007), *U.K. Summer 2007 Floods*, Newark, CA: RMS.

Robinson, V. (1992), 'Move on up: the mobility of Britain's Afro-Caribbean and Asian populations', in J. Stillwell, P. Rees and P. Boden (eds), *Migration Processes and Patterns; Population Redistribution in the United Kingdom*, London: Belhaven, pp. 271–91.

Robinson, V. (1993), 'Race, gender and internal migration within England and Wales', *Environment and Planning A*, **25**(10), 1453–65.

Rogers, A. (1968), *Matrix Analysis of Interregional Population Growth and Distribution*, Berkeley: University of California Press.

Rogers, A. (1995), *Multiregional Demography: Principles, Methods and Extensions*, Chichester: John Wiley.

Rogers, A. (2007), 'Demographic modeling of the geography of migration and population: a multiregional perspective', Boulder: University of Colorado, Institute of Behavioral Science, Population Program, POP2007-02.

Rounsevell, M.D.A. and D.S. Reay (2009), 'Land use and climate change in the UK', *Land Use Policy*, **265**, S160–S169.

Salt, J. (1984), 'Labour transfers during the recession', Durham: Institute of British Geographers Annual Conference.

Salt, J. (1990), 'Organizational labour migration: theory and practice in the United Kingdom', in J.H. Johnson and J. Salt (eds), *Labour Migration*, London: David Fulton, pp. 53–70.

Salt, J. (1991), 'Labour migration and housing in the UK: an overview', in J. Allen and C. Hamnett (eds), *Housing and Labour Markets: Building the Connections*, London: Unwin Hyman.

Salt, J. and R. Kitching (1992), 'The relationship between international and internal migration', in A.G. Champion and A.J. Fielding (eds),

Migration Processes and Patterns: Research Progress and Prospects, London: Belhaven, pp. 148–62.

Sanderson, W.C. and S. Scherbov (2010), 'Remeasuring aging', *Science*, **239**(5997), 1287–8.

Satsangi, M., N. Gallent and M. Bevan (2010), *The Rural Housing Question: Communities and Planning in Britain's Countrysides*, Bristol: Policy Press.

Saunders, P. (1990), *A Nation of Home Owners*, London: Unwin Hyman.

Schipper, L. and I. Burton (eds) (2008), *The Earthscan Reader on Adaptation to Climate Change*, London: Earthscan.

Schwierz, C. et al. (2010), 'Modelling European winter wind storm losses in current and future climate', *Climatic Change*, **101**(3–4), 485–514.

Sharma, V. and G. Hugo (2009), 'Exploring the population–environment nexus: understanding climate change, environmental degradation and migration in Bangladesh', paper, Princeton: IUSSP.

Short, D. and A. Stockdale (1999), 'English migrants in the Scottish countryside: opportunities for rural Scotland?', *Scottish Geographical Journal*, **115**(3), 177–92.

Short, N.K., E.A. Richardson, R. Mitchell and J. Pearce (2011), 'Re-engaging with the physical environment: a health-related environmental classification of the UK', *Area*, **43**(1), 76–87.

Shove, E. (2010), 'Beyond the ABC: climate change policy and theories of social change', *Environment and Planning A*, **42**(6), 1273–85.

Simpson, L. and N. Finney (2009), 'Spatial patterns of internal migration: evidence for ethnic groups in Britain', *Population, Space and Place*, **15**(1), 37–56.

Simpson, S. and E. Middleton (1999), 'Undercount of migration in the UK 1991 Census and its impact on counterurbanization and population projections', *International Journal of Population Geography*, **5**(5), 387–405.

Smallwood, S. and K. Lynch (2010), 'An analysis of patient register data in the Longitudinal Study – what does it tell us about the quality of the data?', *Population Trends*, No. 141, 151–69.

Smith, D. (2002), 'Rural gatekeepers and "greentrifried" Pennine rurality: opening and closing the access gates?', *Social and Cultural Geography*, **3**(4), 447–63 (abstract only).

Smith, D. and L. Holt (2005), 'Lesbian migrants in the "gentrified valley" and "other" geographies of rural gentrification', *Journal of Rural Studies*, **21**(3), 313–22.

Smith, D. and L. Holt (2007), 'Studentification and "apprentice" gentrifiers within Britain's provincial towns and cities: extending the meaning of gentrification', *Environment and Planning A*, **39**(1), 142–61.

Snaith, J. (1990), 'Migration and dual career households', in J.H. Johnson, and J. Salt (eds), *Labour Migration*, London: David Fulton, pp. 155–71.

Spencer, D. (1997), 'Counterurbanization and rural depopulation revisited: landowners, planners and the rural development process', *Journal of Rural Studies*, **13**(1), 75–92.

St Antony's International Review (2010), *New Directions in Climate Change Politics*, University of Oxford: St Antony's College.

Stephenson, J., K. Newman and S. Mayhew (2010), 'Population dynamics and climate change: what are the links?', *Journal of Public Health*, **32**(2), 150–56.

Stern, N. (2008), 'The economics of climate change', *American Economic Review: Papers and Proceedings*, **98**(2), 1–37.

Stillwell, J. (1983), 'Migration between metropolitan and non-metropolitan regions in the UK', Soesterberg: Anglo-Dutch Migration Symposium.

Stillwell, J. (1990), 'Migration analysis based on National Health Service Central Register data: trends and models', London School of Economics: British Society for Population Studies Conference paper.

Stillwell, J. (2010), 'Ethnic population concentration and new migration in London', *Environment and Planning A*, **42**(6), 1439–56.

Stillwell, J. and O. Duke-Williams (2003), 'A new web-based interface to British census of population origin–destination statistics', *Environment and Planning A*, **35**(1), 113–32.

Stillwell, J. and O. Duke-Williams (2005), 'Ethnic population distribution, immigration and internal migration in Britain: what evidence of linkage at the district scale?', University of Kent: BSPS Annual Conference paper.

Stillwell, J. and S. Hussain (2010), 'Exploring the ethnic dimension of internal migration in Great Britain using migration effectiveness and spatial connectivity', *Journal of Ethnic and Migration Studies*, **36**(9), 1381–403.

Stillwell, J., P. Boden and P. Rees (1986), 'Internal migration change in the UK: trends based on NHSCR movement data, 1975–6 to 1985–6', University College London: Regional Science Association Conference paper.

Stillwell, J., P. Rees and P. Boden (1992), 'Internal migration trends: an overview', in J. Stillwell, P. Rees and P. Boden (eds), *Migration Processes and Patterns: Population Redistribution in the United Kingdom*, London: Belhaven, pp. 28–55.

Stillwell, J., P. Rees and O. Duke-Williams (1996), 'Migration between NUTS level 2 regions in the United Kingdom', in P. Rees et al. (eds), *Population Migration in the European Union*, Chichester: John Wiley, pp. 275–307.

Stillwell, J., S. Hussain and P. Norman (2008), 'The internal migration propensities and net migration patterns of ethnic groups in Britain', *Migration Letters*, **5**(2), 135–50.

Stillwell, J., O. Duke-Williams and A. Dennett (eds) (2010), *Technologies for Migration and Commuting Analysis: Spatial Interaction Data Applications*, Hershey, PA: IGI Global.

Stockdale, A. (2002a), 'Towards a typology of out-migration from peripheral areas: a Scottish case study', *International Journal of Population Geography*, **8**(5), 345–64.

Stockdale, A. (2002b), 'Out-migration from rural Scotland: the importance of family and social networks', *Sociologia Ruralis*, **42**(1), 41–64.

Stockdale, A. (2004), 'Rural out-migration: community consequences and individual migrant experiences', *Sociologia Ruralis*, **44**(2), 149–76.

Stockdale, A. (2006a), 'The role of a "retirement transition" in the repopulation of rural areas', *Population, Space and Place*, **12**(1), 1–13.

Stockdale, A. (2006b), 'Migration; pre-requisite for rural economic regeneration?', *Journal of Rural Studies*, **22**(3), 354–66.

Stockdale, A. (2010), 'The diverse geographies of rural gentrification in Scotland', *Journal of Rural Studies*, **26**(1), 31–40.

Stockdale, A. and A. Findlay (2004), 'Rural in-migration: a catalyst for economic regeneration', Glasgow: International Geographical Congress paper.

Stockdale, A., A. Findlay and D. Short (2000), 'The repopulation of rural Scotland: opportunity and threat', *Journal of Rural Studies*, **16**(2), 243–57.

Stripple, J., T. Rayner, R. Hildingsson, A. Jordan and C. Haug (2010), 'Governance choices and dilemmas in a warmer Europe: what does the future hold', in A. Jordan et al. (eds), *Climate Change Policy and the European Union*, Cambridge: Cambridge University Press, pp. 229–50.

Tacoli, C. (2009), 'Crisis or adaptation? Migration and climate change in a context of high mobility', *Environment and Urbanization*, **21**(2), 513–25.

Thomas, A. (1993), 'The influence of wages and house prices on British interregional migration decisions', *Applied Economics*, **25**(9), 1261–8.

Tilling, S.A. (1995), 'The composition of migrant households in new build housing: a "niche" market', Brighton: British Society for Population Studies Conference.

UK: DEFRA (2009), UK climate projections (UKCP09), available at: http://ukclimateprojections.defra.gov.uk/content/view/912/499/; accessed 4 January 2012.

UK: Department of Health, Health Protection Agency (2008), *Health Effects of Climate Change in the UK 2008*, London: DoH.

UK: Government Office for Science (2010), *Land Use Futures: Making the*

Most of Land in the 21st Century, London: Foresight Land Use Futures Project.

UK: Government Office for Science (2011), *The Future of Food and Farming: Challenges and Choices for Global Sustainability*, London: Foresight Project.

UK: Higher Education Statistics Agency (HESA) (2010) (Statistics on non-NI domiciled students at NI HEIs by country of domicile – 2004/05 to 2008/09).

UK: Ministry of Housing and Local Government (MHLG) (1970), *Working Group on Regional Migration Forecasting: Final Report*, London MHLG.

UK: Office of the Deputy Prime Minister (2002), *Development of a Migration Model*, London: Office of the Deputy Prime Minister.

UK: Office of National Statistics (ONS) (2005), 'The UK population at the start of the 21st century', *Population Trends*, No. 122.

UK: Office for Science and Technology (2004), *Future Flooding*, London: Foresight Project.

Unruh, J.D., M.S. Krol and N. Kliot (eds) (2004), *Environmental Change and its Implications for Population Migration*, Dordrecht: Kluwer.

Urry, J. (2011), *Climate Change and Society*, Cambridge: Polity.

Van der Gaag, N., E. Van Imhoff and L. Van Wissen (2000), 'Internal migration scenarios and regional population projections for the European Union', *International Journal of Population Geography*, **6**(1), 1–19.

Vercelloni, C. (2010), 'The crisis of the law of value and the becoming-rent of profit', in A. Fumagalli and S. Mezzadra (eds), *Crisis in the Global Economy*, Los Angeles: Semiotext(e), pp. 85–118.

Vickers, D.W. (2010), *England's Changing Social Geology, 1991–2001*, UPTAP.

Walford, N. (2004), 'Searching for a rural resting place: population in-migration and circulation in Mid-Wales', *Population, Space and Place*, **10**(4), 311–29.

Walford, N. (2007), 'Geographical and geodemographic connections between different types of small area as the origins and destinations of migrants to Mid-Wales', *Journal of Rural Studies*, **23**(3), 318–31.

Warner, K. et al. (2009), *In Search of Shelter: Mapping the Effects of Climate Change on Human Migration and Displacement*, CARE International et al.

Warnes, T. (1992a), 'Migration and the lifecourse', in A.G. Champion and A.J. Fielding (eds), *Migration Processes and Patterns: Research Prospects and Progress*, London: Belhaven Press, pp. 175–87.

Warnes, T. (1992b), 'Temporal and spatial patterns of elderly migration', in J. Stillwell, P. Rees and P. Boden (eds), *Migration Processes and Patterns: Population Redistribution in the United Kingdom*, London: Belhaven, pp. 248–70.

Waters, J., R. Brooks and H. Pimlott-Wilson (2011), 'Youthful escapes? British students, overseas education and the pursuit of happiness', *Social and Cultural Geography*, **12**(5), 455–69.

Weidlich, W. and G. Haag (eds) (1988), *Interregional Migration: Dynamic Theory and Comparative Analysis*, Berlin: Springer-Verlag.

Wheater, H. and E. Evans (2009), 'Land use, water management and future flood risk', *Land Use Policy*, **265**, S251–S264.

Wilkinson, P. (2006), 'Climate change and infectious disease in Africa and the UK', UK Office of Science and Innovation, Foresight paper.

Willekens, F. (2008), 'Models of migration: observations and judgment', in J. Raymer and F. Willekens (eds), *International Migration in Europe: Data, Models and Estimates*, Chichester: Wiley, Chapter 6.

Williams, A. (2008), 'Turning the tide: recognizing climate change refugees in international law', *Law and Policy*, **30**(4), 502–29.

Williams, G. (1985), 'Counter-urbanization and rural social change: a social indicator study of Mid-Wales', University of Manchester: Department of Town and Country Planning, Occasional Paper No. 16.

Wilson, T. and P. Rees (2003), 'Why Scotland needs more than just a new migration policy', *Scottish Geographical Journal*, **119**(3), 191–208.

Wolf, J. et al. (2009), 'Conceptual and practical barriers to adaptation: vulnerability and responses to heat waves in the UK', in W.N. Adger, I. Lorenzoni and K.L. O'Brien (eds), *Adapting to Climate Change: Thresholds, Values, Governance*, Cambridge: Cambridge University Press, pp. 181–96.

World Bank (2009), *World Development Report 2010: Development and Climate Change*, Washington DC: World Bank.

Wright, E. (2010), '2008-based national projections for the United Kingdom and constituent countries', *Population Trends*, No. 139, 91–114.

Index